Reflections on the Sacred Liturgy
Volume I: Lent & Holy Week

Reflections on the Sacred Liturgy

Reflections on the Liturgical Texts, Themes & Scriptures of the Ordinary Form of the Roman Rite

Volume I:
Lent & Holy Week

Fr. Thomas M. Hoisington, S.T.L.

In Hoc Est Caritas Press
Wichita, Kansas

Nihil Obstat
Rev. Joseph M. Gile, S.T.D.
Censor Librorum

Imprimatur
Most Rev. Carl A. Kemme, D.D.
Bishop of Wichita
November 15, 2018 — *Feast of St. Albert the Great*

The *Nihil Obstat* and *Imprimatur* are official declarations that a book or pamphlet is free of doctrinal or moral error. No implication is contained therein that those who have granted the *Nihil Obstat* and the *Imprimatur* agree with the content, opinions or statements expressed.

The covers and the *Reflections on the Sacred Liturgy*
header were designed by Mrs. Kellee Kruse.
The final invocation and the closing prayer of the Litany for Bishops
were composed by Mr. Josh Mansfield.

DEDICATION

This volume is dedicated to my parents,
John Riley Hoisington and Marilyn Jane Kelly Hoisington.

TABLE OF CONTENTS

✠   ✠   ✠

TABLE OF YEARS ACCORDING TO THE THREE-YEAR CYCLE

In the Roman Rite's Ordinary Form of Holy Mass, the Scriptures of the Liturgy of the Word are organized in a three-year cycle for Sundays and most solemnities. The table below shows whether a year's Scriptures for Lent and Holy Week are taken from "Year A", "Year B" or "Year C".

YEAR A	YEAR B	YEAR C
2020	2018	2019
2023	2021	2022
2026	2024	2025
2029	2027	2028
2032	2030	2031

THE WEEK OF ASH WEDNESDAY

Ash Wednesday
Joel 2:12-18 + 2 Corinthians 5:20–6:2 + Matthew 6:1-6,16-18

For our sake he made him to be sin who did not know sin....

In today's First Reading is a verse that's also chanted within one of the antiphons for the Blessing and Distribution of Ashes. *"Between the porch and the altar / let the priests, the ministers of the LORD, weep, / And say, 'Spare, O LORD, your people'"*. This sentence speaks to the Old Testament priest's role among God's People. First, it reveals that the Old Testament priest physically stands between the porch and the altar—between God's People and the place of sacrifice to God—to act as the Prophet Joel describes.

There, the Old Testament priest weeps and cries out on behalf of God's sinful people. While this weeping and crying is not part of his official "job description", which in fact centers on the offering of sacrifice, these actions are clearly bound up with the priest's role as mediator. This is true because the sins of God's People are the reason that he stands where he does: between them and the LORD God, weeping, crying, and finally offering sacrifice.

Yet while this Old Testament background is important, the Church proclaims this verse from the Prophet Joel today in order to point our attention to the priesthood of Jesus Christ.

One phrase in particular from today's Second Reading forces us to reckon with the depth of Jesus' priesthood. What does Saint Paul mean when, speaking about God the Father and the Son, he states: *"For our sake he made him to be sin who did not know*

I

sin"? This saving truth reminds us about three distinct forms of humility that Jesus accepted for our salvation, by which He stands between sinful man and the divine Father.

First, we need to reflect upon God the Son humbling Himself to become human at the Annunciation. Jesus stands between God and man as True God and true man. For scriptural meditation on this saving mystery during Lent, we might use the prologue of St. John's Gospel account or the canticle of Christ's humility found in the second chapter of Philippians.

Then, more than thirty years after His conception, this divine Word made Flesh offered up His life on the Cross. We need to reflect upon Jesus' humility on Calvary. Upon the Cross, Jesus is not an Old Testament priest, crying and weeping and offering a dumb animal in sacrifice. In humility, the Word made Flesh sacrifices His own Body and Blood, soul and divinity. To reflect on this saving mystery, we might use the Passion narrative from any of the four Gospel accounts.

But be careful! Within this second form of Jesus' humility is a third: a mystery that we must not underestimate. Again, in speaking about the Father sending His divine Son to save us, the Apostle declares: *"For our sake he made him to be sin who did not know sin"*.

Often when we meditate upon the Passion of the Christ—say, for example, during the Stations of the Cross—we are impressed by how awfully man's sins affect Jesus. We might imagine the Cross as "containing" our sins, so that the physical weight of Jesus' heavy cross symbolizes the spiritual weight of all mankind's sins. Or we might imagine each lash from the Scourging at the Pillar as representing an individual sin. But while those images may help us meditate upon the meaning of the Passion, St. Paul is saying something even more profound.

God the Father made His divine Son *"to be sin"*: not only to carry sin, or be wounded by sin, but to be made sin. Jesus, who from before time began was God, stands not only in the place of sinners, but in the place of sin. This is where He offers sacrifice as a new and everlasting priest. His stance between merciful grace and man's sins brings together both in Himself, where the former destroys the latter, for us and for our salvation.

2

Thursday after Ash Wednesday
Deuteronomy 13:15-20 + Luke 9:22-25

"Today I have set before you life and prosperity, death and doom."

The setting of the First Reading is the Exodus: a period in Israel's history that corresponds to Lent. As the Israelites wandered for forty years, so the Church walks with Jesus through the desert of Lent. But the Exodus is a journey that courses between two even more significant events: Israel's Passing Over the Red Sea to escape slavery, and Israel's Passing Over the Jordan River to enter the Promised Land.

These three—crossing over the Red Sea, the Exodus, and crossing over the Jordan—can symbolize the whole Christian life: crossing over the Red Sea, our baptism; the Exodus, our Christian life on earth; crossing over the Jordan, our death and entrance into Heaven. The middle of these—the Exodus—corresponds, then, both to the Season of Lent and our Christian life on earth. Each illuminates the other.

"The whole of our Christian life on this earth is a Lenten journey." That claim would seem depressing, but only if we didn't fully appreciate what Lent signifies. If we focus on the deprivation involved in sacrifice, then we miss why we make the sacrifice. If we focus on Lent as an end in itself, we forget that Lent is actually a means to a greater end. Why make sacrifice during Lent? The end of this sacrifice is our rejoicing.

Friday after Ash Wednesday
Isaiah 58:1-9 + Matthew 9:14-15

Would that today you might fast
so as to make your voice heard on high!

Does God need a hearing aid? If not, what accounts for some voices not being heard on high? Since it's not due to some weakness in God's hearing, it must be due to some weakness in our voice.

"Making your voice heard on high" has a two-fold meaning. Objectively, our words have to "befit" God: whatever we ask for must be truly good, capable of imaging God. Were we to ask God for something evil, the petition would fall on deaf ears (metaphorically speaking). Even more than simply not being evil, though, what we ask from or offer to Him also has to be something that God Himself wants. It must be in accord with His providential Will.

Subjectively, we ourselves must truly want and mean what we offer to God. That might seem foolish to suggest: how could we not do so? Yet if we examine our spiritual lives closely, we're likely to see that in the name of being a "good Christian", we go along with what others ask of us, or what we think is expected of us. We offer to God prayers that are not truly rooted in our own human will. This is not "befitting God" either, because in this a Christian presents a false self to God: in prayer—in offering up "my voice" to the Lord—the Christian is meant to give his true self to God.

Saturday after Ash Wednesday
Isaiah 58:9b-14 + Luke 5:27-32

"Those who are healthy do not need a physician, but the sick do."

The older we get, the more often we find ourselves visiting the doctor. The older we grow, the more types of doctors we visit, for ailments of different parts of our bodies. But the average Joe, when he begins to sense a serious sickness, weighs in his mind two counter-balancing dislikes. He weighs the potential for the sickness becoming worse against the hassle of scheduling a trip to the doctor's office, with all that entails both before and afterwards.

Consider all that as an analogy to sin. In today's Gospel Jesus says: *"Those who are healthy do not need a physician, but the sick do."* In the three years of Jesus' public ministry, Jesus often condemns the self-righteous, who don't believe they need a doctor: these are they who say regarding their spiritual lives, "I'm just fine!"

Jesus also shows, in His words and deeds, the need for a good shepherd to reach out to the lamb who is lame, lost or sick. Maybe the lamb even avoids the shepherd and pulls away when it sees the shepherd coming towards him: these are they who say, "Please don't bother about little old me!"

The irony of today's Gospel is that the self-righteous likely need Jesus more than those they accuse of sinfulness. We are all of us—sinful men, women and children—in need of a Savior.

THE FIRST SUNDAY OF LENT

The First Sunday of Lent [Year A]
Genesis 2:7-9; 3:1-7 + Romans 5:12,17-19 + Matthew 4:1-11

A clean heart create for me, O God,
and a steadfast spirit renew within me.

Today's Responsorial is taken from Psalm 51. This psalm is, arguably, the most profound of the seven psalms that are traditionally called the Penitential Psalms [Psalms 6, 32, 38, 51, 102, 130, 143]. For centuries, the seven Penitential Psalms have helped Christians to focus on their need to accept God's mercy, and to practice penance. Here at the beginning of Lent, you might consider copying one of the Penitential Psalms, carrying it with you throughout Lent, and praying it every day. If you're unsure about which to choose, try Psalm 51.

Today's Responsorial is drawn from just eight verses of Psalm 51. Consider each set of verses that the Church sings today between the repetitions of the refrain.

During the first set of verses, we repeatedly petition God. Four times the Church sings of our neediness. But these four needs are of a specific sort. We might say that they're negative in nature. Of course, every need is negative in the sense that we're asking for something we do not have: asking God to fill a void, whether it's an empty pantry or an empty savings account.

But in this first set of verses, we ask God to have mercy on us, to wipe out our offense, to wash us from our guilt, and to cleanse us from our sin. What these four needs have in common is that we're asking God to restore to us something that we once had but have lost.

The second set of verses complements the first. If we admit in the first verses what our need is, the second set of verses helps us answer the question "Why?" Why do we need what we are asking God for? Why did we lose what we once had?

The answer is that we need mercy, and our offenses wiped out, and our guilt washed away, and to be cleansed from sin because each of us has freely chosen to sin. Each of us has sinned, and each of us needs to admit this fact. What the Psalmist in the first set of verses implied, he makes plain in the second. The Psalmist admits in four different ways that he has sinned. He says: "I acknowledge my offense", "my sin is before me always", "Against you only[, God,] have I sinned", and I have "done what is evil in your sight". The Psalmist is willing to admit not only that he has a problem, but that he is the problem.

However, while the first half of today's Responsorial confesses the loss resulting from our human sin, the second rejoices in what God offers us through Divine Mercy. This second half consists of seven petitions, and one promise. But these petitions aren't like those in the first half. The first half's petitions ask God to remove what is negative: to wipe out offense, wash away guilt, and cleanse one of sin.

But now in this second half the Psalmist asks God to restore and sustain what is positive. The Psalmist asks God to restore to him a clean heart, a steadfast spirit, and the joy of God's salvation. He asks God to sustain in him God's presence, His Holy Spirit, and a willing human spirit.

Finally, the Psalmist sings of his end. In the last two verses of today's Responsorial, we hear the goal both of God removing from the Psalmist's life what is negative, and sustaining within him what is positive. Here each of us needs to consider herself or himself to be the Psalmist. What is true of the Psalmist is true of each of us, especially in terms of our Lenten fasting, prayers, and almsgiving.

The final petition of the Psalmist is different from the others within the Responsorial. Now, the Psalmist sings: "O Lord, open my lips." The Psalmist makes this petition with the aim of making God a promise: *"O Lord, open my lips, / and my mouth shall declare your praise."*

Praise of God is the end of mankind. Each of us during Lent needs to keep in mind that all our fasting, prayers, and almsgiving are oriented to this goal. This is what God created Adam and Eve for "in the beginning". The final Adam, Jesus Christ, lives and dies upon this earth to restore to each of us the chance to fulfill this calling from God: to proclaim His praise all our days on this earth, and forever in Heaven.

The First Sunday of Lent [B]
Genesis 9:8-15 + 1 Peter 3:18-22 + Mark 1:12-15

"Repent, and believe in the gospel."

Do you ever feel that you'd enjoy a retreat from the hectic nature of life? Consider the word "retreat". It has both positive and negative connotations. In a positive sense, especially when we speak of a place as a retreat, we're speaking of a place of relaxation and rest. But when we use the word "retreat" as a verb, it implies some sort of weakness and defeat, at least temporarily.

Lent, as a season of our yearly Christian life, is a retreat in both senses. Today's brief Gospel passage is only four verses long. In the first verse we hear: *"The Spirit drove Jesus out into the desert"*. Reflect on the two Persons mentioned in this verse.

"The Spirit" is, of course, the Holy Spirit: the Third Person of the Most Blessed Trinity. There are many ways to describe the Holy Spirit. One of the more famous is to describe the Holy Spirit as the Love of the Father for the Son, and of the Son for the Father. The Father and the Son are, in fact, one in being (that is, of the same divine nature), in and through this very exchange of divine love. Their reciprocal, mutual Love for each other (that is, Each giving Himself to the Other) is the Third Person of the Godhead.

It is this divine Love that *"drove Jesus out into the desert."* That might seem odd to say, that it was divine Love that drove Jesus into an intensely hot, arid place where for almost six weeks He faced temptations from the devil. How can such a driving force be seen as Love?

One of the verses written by the disciple whom Jesus loved clarifies this truth. In his first letter, St. John the Beloved Disciple declares: *"In this is love: / not that we have loved God, but that he loved us / and sent his Son as expiation for our sins"* [1 John 4:10]. Here is the heart of Lent and Easter: the primacy of God the Father's Love. Before any love of ours for God—in fact, in the face of our choice to positively reject God's love—God the Father made a choice to send His Son down from Heaven, into this world of sin, in order to be a sacrificial offering for our sins.

God the Father loves you, not in spite of your sins, but in and through your sins. God the Father, out of love for you, sent His Son into this world. The goal of this mission was for the Son to be crucified on Good Friday, so as to open the gates of Heaven for you. For His part, Jesus accepted in Love the mission His Father gave Him: the mission to be a sacrificial offering on the Cross. It's this Love that drove Jesus into the desert, and to the top of Calvary. The Son's total acceptance of, and self-identification with His Father's love for you as a sinner led to that truth which we heard St. Paul proclaim in the Second Reading on Ash Wednesday: *"For our sake [the Father] made him to be sin who did not know sin, so that we might become the righteousness of God in him"* [2 Corinthians 5:21].

Lent is a retreat with Jesus into the desert of Jesus' love for us: the love in which Jesus becomes our sins. On the one hand, this is a retreat in the negative sense, because it's an honest admission of our human weakness and even defeat, at least temporarily. But we also retreat with Jesus into the desert because He is our Captain. This is the positive sense in which Lent is a retreat. Lent is a blessed time, even a joyful time, because here, in the desert, we are with Jesus. His Presence here makes this time in the desert a thing of beauty.

This desert is for your soul what fire is for gold: a purification. The love of your life is meant to be one with God the Father's Love, just as Jesus' Love is one with the Father's Love. The Holy Spirit is meant to be the driving force of your life, driving you each day into the missions on which the Father sends you, even those that are deserts in your earthly life.

The First Sunday of Lent [C]
Deuteronomy 26:4-10 + Romans 10:8-13 + Luke 4:1-13

"When the devil had finished every temptation, he departed from him for a time."

Jesus Christ in today's Gospel passage faces temptation. Three temptations. Jesus chose not to sin, but He did face these temptations, just as you do. On this first Sunday of Lent, we're not looking directly at death. We're not gazing at Jesus on Calvary. We're gazing at Jesus in the desert. We're reflecting on Jesus dwelling in the midst of temptation. But the importance of looking at Jesus within this desert is to consider how you deal with temptation. Do you deal with temptation as Jesus does in today's Gospel passage? The reason this is important is because if you don't deal with temptation like Jesus, you won't be capable of dealing with death like Jesus. How we deal with suffering determines how we deal with death. Many overlook this important truth of the spiritual life: how we deal with suffering determines how we deal with death.

When we consider, one after the other, the three temptations that Jesus faced, we might not at first see a connection to death. In the first case, you and I as Americans in the 21st century aren't used to thinking of suffering from hunger in connection with death. For us, hunger means not having eaten for ten hours. In the Holy Land of Jesus' day, the connection between hunger and death was very real, and not uncommon. Likewise, in the second case, Jesus is tempted with all of the power of the world. In the Holy Land of Jesus' day, many kingdoms did not recognize an inherent right to life. Life was considered to be in the hands of other human beings, who might or might not allow you to live. In such a savage culture, it was often kill or be killed.

However, it's the third temptation that compels our attention most strongly. After all, the first and second concern earthly goods: food and power. This third temptation is different. It's about something heavenly: not in fact some "thing", but "someone", and not just someone who is good, but the Father who is Goodness Himself. This third temptation concerns the goodness of God the Father.

Here in the desert, the devil appeals not to Jesus' desire for food or power, but to Jesus' desire for the protection—the loving, providential care—of God the Father. The devil is very logical in pointing out, *"If you are the Son of God... [God the Father] 'will command his angels... to guard you....'"* This third temptation, of course, is only the foreshadow of the Cross on Calvary.

Do you imagine that on Good Friday, as Jesus spent those three hours nailed to the Cross, that the devil repeated the third desert temptation? Do you imagine that the devil whispered to Jesus, *"If you are the Son of God,"* ask God the Father to take you *"down from here, for it is written: 'He will command his angels concerning you, to guard you....'"*

But no angels guarded Jesus from the blows of His executioners, from the Crown of thorns, from the nails that pierced His Body, or from falling three times on the dirty Way of the Cross.

During this coming week—the first full week of Lent—consider this third temptation. Consider Jesus' relationship with God the Father, and the Father' decision not to care for His only-begotten Son by shielding Him from the Cross. Consider the truth that all of Jesus' suffering and His death reflect His love for His Father, and His trust in the Father's Providential will. Trust in the Father's love for you, and His desire that you serve Him by following Jesus to Calvary.

WEEKDAYS OF THE FIRST WEEK OF LENT

Monday of the First Week of Lent
Leviticus 19:1-2,11-18 + Matthew 25:31-46

"Amen, I say to you, whatever you did for one of these least brothers of mine, you did for me."

In today's Gospel passage, Jesus describes a real, future event: the Last Judgment that will take place at the end of time. To describe this future event, He uses the metaphor of sheep and goats. Then Jesus describes the difference between these sheep and goats. This difference is one of the most important teachings of the Gospel.

Historically, there have been many disputes between Protestants and Catholics about the role of faith, and the role of good works, in the life of the Christian. By which of them do we enter heaven? The Catholic Church, from the first century, to the sixteenth century, to today, has taught that—if you make it to Heaven—it will be because you bore both faith and good works. Each is indispensable, not only for personal salvation. Each of them is indispensable for the perduring of the other. Faith does not perdure unless it is manifested through good works, while works without faith do not lead to eternal salvation.

Jesus' description today of the Last Judgment—which He spoke two days before the Passover during Holy Week [see Matthew 25-26]—makes it seemingly impossible to deny the role of good works in the Christian's entrance into Heaven. Nonetheless, beyond any disputes that might still go on today, we need before disputing the meaning of the Christian Faith simply to live the Christian Faith. Jesus calls us to live the Christian Faith by seeking Him in the disguise of the poor, in all the forms that poverty takes.

Tuesday of the First Week of Lent
Isaiah 55:10-11 + Matthew 6:7-15

"If you forgive men their transgressions, your heavenly Father will forgive you."

When we look at the *Our Father* in the context of Saint Matthew's Gospel account, it's striking that the first topic that Jesus discusses after handing over this prayer to His disciples is the forgiveness of sins. This is not surprising, but it is striking. The *Our Father* is sometimes considered to be a compendium of the Gospel. So then, after giving us the "treasury" of the Lord's Prayer, the Lord begins to teach by discussing the reality of sin.

Challenge those who dismiss either Lenten penance, or the Christian belief in sin itself. But recognize, at the same time, that Jesus' words following today's Gospel passage point us not to our own sins, or to the divine Love that we see when we look at the crucifix.

Jesus points us outwards, to *"those who trespass against us"*. As Christians, our spiritual growth is defined not merely by our own sins, nor even—in the end—only by God's love. In the end, we are defined by the manner in which we turn to others and forgive them as we have been forgiven by God the Father, by means of the very love by which He has forgiven us.

Wednesday of the First Week of Lent
Jonah 3:1-10 + Luke 11:29-32

"Just as Jonah became a sign to the Ninevites, so will the Son of Man be to this generation."

In Catholic theology, typology is the study of types. A type is something (usually, someone) who foreshadows or pre-figures some future thing. A type of a person can foreshadow by means of some personal quality (for example, the physical strength of Samson might be said to foreshadow the spiritual strength of Christ; or the wisdom of Solomon, the Wisdom who is Christ). A person who is a type can also foreshadow through the events of a narrative, as in today's readings, where the narrative involving Jonah foreshadows the narrative of Holy Week.

Jonah foreshadows Jesus Christ. We see many things about Jonah and the events surrounding him that point to Jesus. But Jesus Himself mentions one thing in particular. He mentions for whom Jonah was a sign: *"...Jonah became a sign to the Ninevites."* So will Jesus Himself, he explains, become a sign "to this generation."

So He is for our generation, also. We can look back, then, to the Ninevites, as if looking in a mirror, and ask how our lives might be reflected in theirs. The *Book of the Prophet Jonah* is, in fact, very short. It is only four chapters long, and the chapters are 16, 11, 10 and 11 verses long, for a total of just 48 verses! Take some extra time over the next day, then, to read all 48 verses of the *Book of Jonah*.

Thursday of the First Week of Lent
Esther C:12,14-16,23-25 + Matthew 7:7-12

"Do to others whatever you would have them do to you. This is the law and the prophets."

Today Jesus gives us the "Golden Rule". He gives a new focus for our moral choices, asking us to see ourselves in others. If we saw another person as "our self", we wouldn't make many of the choices that we do.

Unfortunately, we often don't look on others as "our self", and so Jesus, knowing how greatly we need help, offers a further perspective to help us in making moral decisions. Jesus asks us to think as a father thinks. More specifically, He is asking us to think as God the Father thinks.

How and why does God the Father give you gifts? He does not give you gifts in order for you to become popular. He does not give you gifts in order to make you more attractive. He does not give you gifts in order to make your life smooth. These things are not bad, but they are beside the point. Beside the point of life, that is.

God the Father gives you the gifts you need to accomplish your vocation: your reason for being in this world. If we believe this, then we will accept what God the Father gives us as gifts that are means to that end. It's really no more complicated than what the *Catechism* taught us as children. "God made us to know Him, to love Him and to serve Him in this world, so as to be happy with Him in the next."

Friday of the First Week of Lent
Ezekiel 18:21-28 + Matthew 5:20-26

"You have heard that it was said...."

In today's Gospel passage, from very early in the Sermon on the Mount, Jesus gives His first example of the "New Law": the Law of Love, in contrast to Israel's understanding of the Law of Moses. The examples that Jesus gives in this section of the Sermon on the Mount have a consistent structure: **"You have heard that it was said.... But I say to you...."**

As a background to today's example, consider that our Christian Faith teaches that sins come only from the human will. There are indeed sins that rise out of the soil of anger, fear, boredom, and other emotions. But those emotions are not the sins. The "sins of anger" (or "of fear", or "of boredom") are the choices that we freely make when we allow these emotions to dictate our thoughts, words, and actions (that is to say, when we match our actions to our emotions).

Consider carefully what Jesus says: He does not say,

"Whoever is angry with his brother is sinning." Jesus says that when anger is within a person, that person will be *"liable to judgment"*, meaning that the freely chosen actions that flow out of a person filled with anger will be judged. That person may be judged innocent. Regardless, a person with anger in his soul will be held liable for his choices, not only if he kills out of anger, but even if he speaks or thinks in anger.

Note also that emotions come and go, but our choices remain. Among the many true "sins of anger" (again, free choices that flow from a soul experiencing anger), one of the more powerful is the free choice to "nurture" or "nurse" the emotion of anger. In a normal human life, anger can leave one's life just as quickly as it enters. But often, a person wants to use this emotion as a source of what he falsely considers a form of "strength". This active nurturing of anger is a true and common sin.

With all this in mind, and in light of the Cross of Jesus Christ, we can today reflect on this question: Do I ask God merely to take away my anger, or to help me act justly in the face of my anger?

Saturday of the First Week of Lent
Deuteronomy 26:16-19 + Matthew 5:43-48

"But I say to you, love your enemies...."

Today's Gospel passage is from the first third of the Sermon on the Mount. This "inaugural address" is recorded (in full) only in *Matthew*, in chapters 5-7. Today's Gospel passage forms part of a series in chapter 5 of five contrasts between the commands of the Law and Jesus' commands to love. Each contrast uses a variation of the form, *"You have heard that it was said.... But I say to you."*

The contrast presented in today's Gospel passage is the last of these five contrasts. You could easily argue that Jesus saved the hardest for last! How are we to love our enemies? The simple answer is: "Like Jesus on Calvary."

We might begin by asking how our enemies got to be our enemies in the first place. Sinners gain enemies because of their sins. So one way to shorten the list of our enemies is to sin less.

Jesus, of course, was sinless, but still had plenty of enemies. In fact, Jesus had enemies for just the opposite reason that sinners do: because of His unwillingness to compromise with evil. To whatever extent we may, through God's grace, bear holiness in our own lives, we too will win enemies. These enemies we must love unto the Cross.

THE SECOND SUNDAY OF LENT

The Second Sunday of Lent [A]
Genesis 12:1-4 + 2 Timothy 1:8-10 + Matthew 17:1-9

"And behold, Moses and Elijah appeared to them, conversing with him."

The Luminous Mysteries of the Rosary shed light upon who Jesus is, and upon His mission on earth. The scene narrated in today's Gospel passage is the fourth Luminous Mystery. What does this mystery of Jesus' Transfiguration reveal about Him and His earthly mission, and how does this mystery help us along our own Lenten pilgrimage?

Start at the end of the Gospel passage. Jesus commands Peter, James, and John not *"to tell the vision [of the Transfiguration] to anyone until the Son of Man has been raised from the dead."* We can gather why the apostles must wait to tell about the Transfiguration from the way Peter responds to it. Jesus likely feared that others, when hearing of the Transfiguration, would think as Peter did when he said: *"Lord, it is good that we are here. If you wish, I will make three tents here"*. Peter wants them all to remain where they are. He doesn't want this moment to pass. But the moment must pass. The glory of the Transfiguration is a means to the end that is Jesus' death.

Consider the company that Jesus keeps high on that mountain. The three chief apostles witness the transfigured Jesus conversing with Moses and Elijah. Moses represents the Law of the Old Testament, while Elijah represents its prophets. Jesus, with face and clothes like the sun and light, in the midst of Moses and Elijah, evokes a promise that Jesus had made at

21

the beginning of His Sermon on the Mount: *"Do not think that I have come to abolish the law or the prophets. I have come not to abolish but to fulfill"* [Matthew 5:17]. The vision of the Transfiguration helps us see what glory there will be when this fulfillment comes to pass, and helps us see what this fulfillment demands. But that fulfillment is not here and now on this mountain.

Jesus only hints at His fulfillment through His command to the apostles: *"Do not tell the vision to anyone until the Son of Man has been raised from the dead."* These are the very last words of today's Gospel passage. We don't hear the apostles' response to Jesus speaking about rising from the dead. Yet even were you to open your bible and read what comes next, you'd find little to suggest that these apostles understand the Passion, death and Resurrection that are to come.

You and I, of course, know "the rest of the story". You and I know that four weeks from now we will celebrate the death and Resurrection of Jesus, including His triumphal entry into Jerusalem, His solemn institution of the Holy Eucharist, and His bitter Way of the Cross. You and I wouldn't try to build three tents here and now on this mountain, keeping ourselves from the journey that leads to Easter.

Still, while it's true that we know what happens next, aren't you and I like these three apostles? We have no way of knowing what world events might shake the landscapes of our own nation, and of those nations that are friend and foe. We cannot know if severe weather might destroy the property and homes of loved ones and even of ourselves. We cannot possibly know whether a loved one, or ourselves, will be stricken during the next four weeks by a cancer, stroke, or heart attack, or by a personal calamity such as betrayal, as Jesus experienced not long after giving the Eucharist to the Church at the Last Supper. Such calamities, hardships and suffering easily tempt us not to move forward in life.

No matter what way in which you are challenged to move forward in faith, listen to God the Father speaking in today's Gospel passage. He speaks from the clouds: *"This is my beloved Son, with whom I am well pleased; listen to him."* The Father helps us to see that the One who stands in glory in this vision, who will fulfill the Law and the Prophets, is not just a New Moses and a New Elijah. He is God's own Son. His glory is His own, and it's by His own divine strength that He will fulfill the Law and the Prophets, even if the form of that fulfillment—the form of the Cross—is not yet in view. Jesus by His divine strength wants to strengthen us in the midst of our own sufferings. Wherever we fall from the weight of our crosses, Jesus wants to meet us with His grace, comforting us with His words, *"Rise, and do not be afraid."*

The Second Sunday of Lent [B]
Genesis 22:1-2,9,10-13,15-18 + Romans 8:31-34 + Mark 9:2-10

So they kept the matter to themselves, questioning what rising from the dead meant.

In today's Gospel passage we hear about the Transfiguration of Jesus: the great vision of Christ glorified, which foreshadows the Resurrection. Peter, James, and John were invited to see the real reason for following this man, Jesus from Nazareth. At this point in their lives, the disciples had been following Jesus for quite some time. Yet on this day when Jesus was transfigured before Peter, James and John, Jesus' suffering, death, and resurrection were still quite some ways in the future.

In following Jesus around, these disciples had already endured many trials, and yet at this point they still weren't sure where they were going with Jesus. They surely weren't expecting Jesus to die the death of a criminal on the Cross, much less rise from the dead. These disciples had simply been called by a fellow Jew who happened to be a carpenter, and who seemed to possess miraculous powers. It was amazing to follow such a man, but where was it leading them? Jesus' transfiguration offered a hint.

Turn then to your own spiritual life. If you were given the chance to see into your future, would you take it? Would you change the way you pray, or change what you pray for, if you knew what the future holds? It's possible that a glimpse of the future that God has in store would make you a better person. It's possible that a glimpse of your future—the path by which God is asking you to follow Jesus—would make you pray more seriously.

However, for Peter, James and John in today's Gospel passage, seeing Jesus transfigured, and seeing him speaking with the ancient Jewish prophets Moses and Elijah, left them with more questions than answers. We ought to consider that this is true in our spiritual lives, as well, whether we want it to be true or not: namely, that oftentimes, each answer that God gives us raises several new questions. Sometimes, we ought to think twice before asking God for answers.

Take St. Peter as an example. Jesus had chosen Peter to lead His Church on earth, yet Peter completely misunderstands why Jesus had revealed His glory to them. *"Rabbi,"* Peter exclaims, *"it is good that we are here! Let us make three tents."* In other words, he's saying, "Let's pitch tent here and stay awhile."

It's hard to fault Peter for saying this. Each of us, when we find a winning horse in life, wants to bet on it. There are more than enough things in life that we're unsure about. So why should the disciples leave the mountain? The Transfiguration was the greatest vision of Jesus that they'd ever seen. For our part, if any one of us came home some afternoon and found Jesus there, wouldn't we be happy for the rest of our lives to have Him dwell under our roof?

But that's not how Jesus works, either in today's Gospel passage, or in your spiritual life. As Jesus does continually throughout the Gospel, He corrects Peter. He basically says to Peter: "You cannot stop and stay on this peak, because I am not going to stop here." Of course, that's exactly what Jesus did: He left behind the glory of the Transfiguration, and kept on walking the path that would take Him to Calvary.

"As they were coming down from the mountain, [Jesus] *charged"* Peter, James, and John *"not to relate what they had seen to anyone"* until after Jesus had risen from the dead. In other words, Jesus told them, "Don't preach the glory of the Resurrection before its time." Or He might have said: "Don't put the cart before the horse", which is to say, "Don't put Easter Sunday ahead of Good Friday."

Jesus is not to be worshipped as someone completely unlike us. It is in His humanity, His "lowly flesh," that He is glorified. Likewise, it's in our humanity—especially through our weaknesses—that we bear inside us opportunities to allow God's grace to work within us. We do not have to experience miraculous visions in order to follow Jesus faithfully.

The Second Sunday of Lent [C]
Genesis 15:5-12,17-18 + Philippians 3:14—4:1 + Luke 9:28-36

"This is my chosen Son; listen to him."

"This is my chosen Son; listen to him." These words of God the Father seem very simple and straightforward, like God Himself. These words could be used as a summary of the Christian spiritual life, and of the Christian moral life. We focus on both of these—our spiritual life and our moral life—during this Season of Lent, so it's no surprise that the Church proclaims the Gospel of the Transfiguration every year on the Second Sunday of Lent. What is surprising is how difficult we find it to conform ourselves to this request of the Father. We find it difficult and complicated to delve into a deep prayer life, and to abandon our habitual sins. Yet the reason it's so difficult is because we ignore the Father: we do not listen to Jesus Christ.

A life that is heroically virtuous and devoutly prayerful draws its strength from three sources. The first is human nature and its natural virtues such as prudence, justice, temperance and fortitude. These are virtues that even the ancient pagans before Jesus recognized, practiced, and drew strength from to pursue their personal goals. The second is the three supernatural virtues of faith, hope and charity, which can only come from God, and can only lead to God. There are, of course, worldly forms of faith, hope and love, but those are not what the Scriptures point us towards. The third is grace, pure and simple: God's life, God's love, God's strength. This is actually the third supernatural virtue—the virtue of charity—but it is given to us in many different forms.

All of these sources of strength help us. But on this Second Sunday of Lent, focus your attention on one particular way of drawing strength for your life as a Christian: namely, the life of prayer.

One way to describe prayer is to say that it is "communication" with God. Real communication, whether in marriage or in one's relationship with God, involves both listening and speaking. A marriage where only one spouse

26

speaks—where's there's no dialogue, but only monologues—will not grow to its intended fullness. A relationship with God where only the Christian speaks becomes empty: not because God has left, but because the Christian has drowned out God's voice.

Our First Reading helps us here. We learn from the covenant relationship between God and Abram that prayer, while often a dialogue, is meant to lead into silence. Not just our human silence: not just quieting our human voice so as to hear God's. The trance that Abram enters represents the deepest stage of prayer: what in our Catholic tradition is called mystical prayer. This deepest level of prayer is not just for lofty saints like Saint Teresa of Avila. This deepest level of prayer is the goal of prayer for every Christian, as the Council Fathers at Vatican II said. This deepest stage of prayer is a foretaste of Heaven. That is to say, if you and I reach Heaven, this is what we will experience there: a mystical relationship with God. The question isn't whether you are meant for this. The question is whether—given that you persevere in God's grace—you will experience it only in Heaven, or even on earth grasp some glimpse of it in your prayer.

The trick is that to be disposed to deeper levels of prayer, we have to root out of our souls more thoroughly the selfishness that lies underneath the surface of our lives. So you can see at this point that the Christian life is like the chicken and the egg: the relationship between our moral life and our spiritual life is complex. Each builds upon the other, and the sins in the one area make it easier to commit sins in the other.

Maybe to take one simple step forward this Lent, in either our moral life or our spiritual life, we should keep in mind the simple phrase of Saint Paul in today's Second Reading: *"our citizenship is in heaven."* God has created you for Heaven, not for earth. Like Jesus at the Transfiguration, we cannot remain here and rest. We have an exodus to make, a pilgrimage to make, and Christ is our guide, if we listen to Him.

WEEKDAYS OF THE SECOND WEEK OF LENT

Monday of the Second Week of Lent
Daniel 9:4-10 + Luke 6:36-38

"Be merciful, just as your Father is merciful."

Perhaps the simplest form of Lectio Divina that we can practice is to search out a single verse from the Scriptures of the day's Mass, to commit it to memory, and then to repeat it to oneself often throughout the day. In today's Gospel passage, there is a particular verse that almost jumps out at us. *"Be merciful, just as your Father is merciful."*

But as is often the case with a particular verse of Sacred Scripture, there are different emphases that one can make in reciting that same verse. Regarding this verse from today's Gospel passage, for example, you might well pause for emphasis when you come to the two words in the middle of the sentence: *"...just as...."* These two words—as small as they are—remind us of something central to Lent, and to being a Christian.

We hear a plea for the Father's mercy in today's Responsorial Psalm, the refrain of which is: *"Lord, do not deal with us according to our sins"* [based on Psalm 103:10]. We give thanks during Lent that God the Father—through His Son—has not dealt with us according to our sins. We ask the Lord during Lent to open our hearts to the Gift of Jesus' Cross.

We see the Father's mercy in the person of Jesus. On the Cross, we see how merciful God the Father is. So we beg God, through His grace, to help us be towards others just as merciful as Our Father is to them and us alike.

Tuesday of the Second Week of Lent
Isaiah 1:10,16-20 + Matthew 23:1-12

"You have but one Father in heaven."

Sometimes this verse is quoted against Catholics, who address their priests as "Father". However, you don't at the same time hear the New Testament *Letter to Philemon* quoted, where Saint Paul says, *"I appeal to you for my child, Onesimus, whose father I have become in my imprisonment"* [verse 10]. Are these words of Saint Paul un-biblical, and un-Christian?

Or ought we, rather, look at today's Gospel passage in its own scriptural context? Scripturally, the first and last verses of today's Gospel passage help us see the meaning of Jesus' words: *"You have but one Father in heaven."*

Jesus begins by pointing out the contradiction of the scribes and Pharisees. They legitimately hold the *"chair of Moses"*, but the choices of their lives are illegitimate. They do not practice what they preach. These first words of the passage present the problem.

The passage's last words present the answer: *"Whoever humbles himself will be exalted."* Everything in between is a means to this end. Today, then, reflect on this question: "How often do I pray specifically to God the Father, and nurture my relationship with Him as if I were indeed a humble child of His?"

Wednesday of the Second Week of Lent
Jeremiah 18:18-20 + Matthew 20:17-28

"My chalice you will indeed drink...."

As does yesterday's, today's Gospel passage focuses our attention on the virtue of humility. When Jesus prophesies to James and John *"My chalice you will indeed drink"*, we may wince, given that we know "the rest of the story". We know, although

James and John don't, that Jesus' *"chalice"* is His sorrowful Passion and Death. These words should provoke true pity in us for what James and John are asking.

However, the meaning of today's Gospel passage is more than simply, "Be careful what you wish for...." Nor is the meaning limited only to James and John as apostles: Jesus' words in this verse are for each of His followers, including yourself.

Every one of us, as a Christian, ought to strive to make James and John's petition our own: not unknowingly—as their mother asked—but knowingly. Knowing that Jesus' *"chalice"* is the Cup of Suffering, which collected His own Precious Blood from the Cross, we ask Jesus out of love to let us drink from His chalice. The fruit of this chalice will strengthen us to walk with Jesus on our own ways of the Cross, and through them to eternal life.

Thursday of the Second Week of Lent
Jeremiah 17:5-10 + Luke 16:19-31

He is like a tree planted beside the waters....

During the Season of Lent we often meditate on the image of a desert: whether the Sinai Desert, through which the Israelites wandered for forty years after their Passover, or the wilderness where Jesus prayed and fasted for forty days before His public life began, leading to the Passover of His Death and Resurrection. We might well consider Calvary to be a desert, also: if not physically, then morally and spiritually, since no place on earth in human history has ever been as close to Hell as Calvary.

By contrast, the person whose hope is the Lord *"is like a tree planted beside the waters"*. This contrast leads us to consider the Old Testament types of the Red Sea, the water flowing from the rock at Meribah (as we heard yesterday in the Office of Readings), and the Jordan River. All of these are types of the waters of the Baptism that flows from Christ.

One of the truths that we see in meditating upon the image from Jeremiah of *"a tree planted beside the waters"* is that it is rooted—physically and metaphysically—in the soil. The "waters", perhaps from a river, soak through the soil, into the roots, and so nourish the tree. So in the light of Jeremiah's words from our First Reading today—and its echoes in the Responsorial—you might ask yourself in what ways you can tend to this soil, to foster the growth of the tree of life within your soul.

Friday of the Second Week of Lent
Genesis 37:3-4,12-13,17-28 + Matthew 21:33-43,45-46

"This is the heir. Come, let us kill him and acquire his inheritance."

Saint Thomas More said that no heresy is all falsehood. In a similar way, there is no sin that does not have either a good object as its goal, or an intention that is believed to be good. Of course, subjectively believing an intention to be good does not make it objectively good.

This is seen in today's parable about the vineyard owner. We see a spectacularly poor logic on display in the reasoning of the vineyard workers. How could they imagine that by killing the owner's son, they would acquire his inheritance? The father was still alive: did the workers imagine that the owner would forgive them for killing his son, and bestow upon them the vineyard? Or did they plan to take the vineyard by force? If the latter, they should have killed the father in addition to the son, according to their own twisted logic.

Every one of our sins is an offense against Jesus Christ, the Father's only-begotten, who called Himself *"the way and the truth and the life"* [John 14:6]. We imagine that our sins will bring us a greater, longer or more satisfying life. Yet Jesus teaches us that we can only acquire His inheritance of divine Life through the Cross.

Saturday of the Second Week of Lent
Micah 7:14-15,18-20 + Luke 15:1-3,11-32

"'...your brother was dead and has come to life again'".

Many of the parables found only in the Gospel account of St. Luke are noted for demonstrating the virtues of mercy and compassion. Most noteworthy among these is the parable we hear in today's Gospel passage: the Parable of the Prodigal Son. An icon or painting of the father embracing the returning son is often on view in confessionals or, during Lent, in vestibules, so closely identified is this parable with the virtues of mercy and compassion.

We usually consider the word "prodigal" to mean "wasteful". In addition to this primary meaning, however, the word "prodigal" has another meaning: "lavish". The words "wasteful" and "lavish" have something in common, of course, but we think of "wasteful" as being inherently negative, while being "lavish" can sometimes be positive.

The prodigal son has a prodigal father. This father in the parable is an icon of God the Father. The prodigal son's father spares no expense is rejoicing over his son's return. In this he symbolizes the joy of God the Father in one of his wayward children turning away from sin and back towards Him. The prodigal father extends his mercy, however, not only to those who turn back from a sinful life, but also to those—like the older brother—who themselves refuse to show mercy.

32

THE THIRD SUNDAY OF LENT

The Third Sunday of Lent [A]
Exodus 17:3-7 + Romans 5:1-2,5-8 + John 4:5-42

"'Is the LORD in our midst or not?'"

This year on the Third, Fourth, and Fifth Sundays of Lent, our Gospel passage comes from the *Gospel according to Saint John*. Saint John's Gospel account differs from *Matthew*, *Mark*, and *Luke* in many ways. One of the unique things about *John* that we will hear during these three Sundays is that *John* often expresses double meanings through the words and works of Jesus. For example, when Jesus cures a blind man, the evangelist goes out of his way to show how that cure—besides being a physical miracle—is also a sign that Jesus can cure a person's spiritual blindness. Similarly, in *John* Jesus speaks with Nicodemus late at night about being **"born from above"** [John 3:3], which Nicodemus misunderstands as meaning **"born again"** [John 3:4].

In today's Gospel passage from *John* is another conversation. Jesus meets a Samaritan woman, an outcast who represents every human sinner. At the very beginning of the conversation, Jesus asks her for a drink of water. Think about this: Jesus Christ, who is God, asks the outcast for what He does not have. Immediately, this sounds strange, that an all-powerful God would ask a sinful woman for a drink. Why would He do this?

Surely if Jesus had wanted He could have worked a miracle greater than the one God had worked through Moses in the desert, bringing water from the rock at Massah and Meribah. So given His divine omnipotence, what does Jesus need with this sinful Samaritan woman? What does Jesus need with us? He needs nothing. But He asks the outcast for something that He does not have, in order to give her something greater. Although Jesus needs nothing, He wants a great deal: that is to say, He wants every human soul to be His.

Here *John*'s double meaning begins to emerge. Jesus asks the outcast for what he does not have. He does not have the outcast's soul. The Samaritan woman has chosen, over the years, to keep her soul to herself, to use herself and others for her own desires. But God wants her soul. Of course God could always have anything He wants, just as He could have produced a river in the desert to quench His thirst. But God chooses, at the moment a human life begins, to give that person freedom: the freedom to love Him completely, which in turn means the freedom to leave Him completely.

Each of us sinners chooses to use his freedom for his own sake, to serve his own needs and desires. But the more a person serves himself, the darker, the deader, and the harder his heart becomes. God, of course, is always free to take away our sins without our confessing them, but if He were to do that, He would also take away our freedom. God uses His divine freedom to withhold forgiveness, so that we may use our human freedom to ask His forgiveness.

Jesus, throughout His dialogue with the outcast, works at drawing forth a confession from the depths of her sinful heart, just as He asks her to draw water from the depths of the well. When the outcast finally recognizes her need for something greater than this world's pleasures, she turns to God. From Him she seeks the joy which only He can pour down from heaven, the grace that floods the soul for the first time in the waters of Baptism.

Those of us who have already been washed in Baptism also admit our sins during Lent, availing ourselves of the Sacrament of Confession. But we might ask ourselves, "Why do we confess our sins?" After all, God already has knowledge of our sins. Then again, why would Jesus in today's Gospel passage need to ask for something He already has access to?

We see that Jesus, in asking something of the Samaritan

woman, is in fact offering her something. In her conversation with Jesus, she comes to recognize her own sinfulness, and from her heart flow tears of sorrow for her sins. From the hardened heart of an outcast flows her human love for God, and God in return offers a share in divine, eternal love. Tears of sorrow prepare souls to receive the flood-waters of God's Divine Mercy.

God is working to call each of us into a conversation with Him. Jesus wants to speak to each of us, heart to heart. Each of us has the opportunity to approach Him and offer Him our sinful selves, knowing that there is no heart so hardened by sin that God does not want to draw human love from it, and fill it with His own divine love.

The Third Sunday of Lent [B]
Exodus 20:1-17 + 1 Corinthians 1:22-25 + John 2:13-25

"Destroy this temple, and in three days I will raise it up."

On the middle three Sundays of Lent this year, the Gospel passage comes from the *Gospel according to Saint John*. If one of your Lenten resolutions is to spend more time reading the Bible, I would strongly recommend that you read the *Gospel according to St. John*. If you have not chosen to read the Bible as a Lenten practice, I would strongly recommend that you read the *Gospel according to St. John*.

As you know, among the four Gospel accounts, *John* is unique. *Matthew*, *Mark*, and *Luke* have much in common with each other. Unlike those three Gospel accounts, though, which are very "down-to-earth", John uses images, symbols, and events from Jesus' life that highlight Jesus' divinity. In fact, the bulk of *John* is divided into two parts: the first half describes various signs that Jesus performed during the three years of His public ministry. These signs draw a portrait of Jesus as a worker of wonders. It's easy to understand, reading the first chapters of John, why people would have become His followers.

Even in the scenes in these early chapters of *John* where Jesus is not working a miracle, His actions show Him as completely given over to the Will of God the Father. There was no compromise in Jesus' life. In today's Gospel passage, for example, we don't see Jesus working a miracle. But His actions are still a sign that point to Him being completely given over to the work of His Father.

Lots of people in Jesus' day were fed up with the materialism and commercialism that had crept into the practices of the Temple in Jerusalem. The Temple was the holiest place in the entire world for Jews, and today's Gospel passage is set at the time of the Jewish Passover, the holiest time of the year. In the same way that Christmas, one of the holiest times of the Christian year, is plagued today by commercialism, so was the time of Passover during Jesus' life.

One of the obligations of a faithful Jew in Jesus' day and age was to go to Jerusalem at the time of Passover, and offer a sacrifice in the Temple: those who were wealthy offered an entire ox or sheep; those with less means offered turtledoves. This was a formal, legal obligation. So during Passover there was a large market for these animals, and within this market many abuses had developed. Jesus undoubtedly had many people cheering for Him as He told off the corrupt Jewish officials and the money-makers in the Temple.

But you have to wonder how many people continued to cheer for Him when the Jews asked for a sign from Jesus, and He replied, *"Destroy this temple and in three days I will raise it up"*? Many bystanders were likely baffled. Some probably became angry at Jesus: after all, here He had been purifying the Temple, and now He wanted to destroy it? The Scriptures tell us that Jesus' own disciples only came to understand his words after His Resurrection, so you can imagine what those who did not know Jesus well thought of these words.

In any case, when we look at the entire course of Saint John's Gospel account, the meaning of Jesus' words becomes apparent. Jesus wasn't talking about destroying the Temple in Jerusalem that was made of stone. As necessary as the cleansing of the Temple was, Jesus was speaking about a completely different destruction, and a completely different temple. Jesus was speaking about the temple not made by human hands, but rather His own Body, born of a virgin. Along this line, in the same way that these words of Jesus refer to His own physical Body that was crucified, these words also refer to the Church, which is the Mystical Body of Christ: the body of which each of us is one member.

The Temple in Jerusalem, made of stone, was itself a foreshadowing of the Church, and Jesus' righteous anger against the corruption of the Temple in Jerusalem is a sign of Jesus' desire for the Church herself to be pure. But the Body of the Church is only as pure as each of her members. That is why, as a Church, all of us are given the gift of the Season of Lent, so that each member of the Church can put himself to the spiritual cleansing to which Jesus put the Jerusalem Temple.

The Third Sunday of Lent [C]
Exodus 3:1-8,13-15 + 1 Corinthians 10:1-6,10-12 + Luke 13:1-9

"Sir, leave it for this year also... it may bear fruit in the future. If not, you can cut it down."

Both in the Old Testament and the New Testament, gardens, plants and trees of all sorts are used as symbols of growth—and decay—in the spiritual life. The very first story of the Bible takes place in a garden called Eden. Today in the Gospel, Jesus tells us a parable along similar lines.

Your spiritual life is the fig tree, and you are the gardener. Your spiritual life is planted in the LORD's orchard. What we have to come to grips with is the fact that we are accountable to the Lord, just as in today's parable the gardener is accountable to the owner of the orchard. We are accountable for bearing spiritual fruit in our lives on this earth.

That's why we're here on this earth. If we believed, as some of our fellow Christians do, that the entire point of our relationship with Christ is to be "saved", then we would be better off dying as soon as we're baptized. But the whole truth is that salvation comes to us only at the end of our life on this earth, if we have been faithful to tending our spiritual life and bearing fruit in its many settings: the relationship between spouses, and the decisions they make together; relationships between parents and their children, and the many situations in which children are called to respect their parents and obey their decisions; relationships between employers and employees, among neighbors and friends, and so on.

This season of Lent is a natural time to imagine, in the context of our own spiritual lives, a conversation taking place like the one in Jesus' parable. The LORD asks you each year in this season of Lent to offer an account of your spiritual life. And you, in reply, should be willing to make the gardener's words your own: *"Sir, leave it for this year also, and I shall cultivate the ground around it and fertilize it...."*

There are two things that the gardener promises to do here: cultivate and fertilize. The cultivation of our spiritual life means to use every tool at our disposal to build up the graces on which God has founded our lives, as well as the graces that He wants to bestow upon us every new day of our life. There are many ways to fertilize our spiritual life, but during Lent especially, one of them is to acknowledge that—if you'll pardon the expression—even the manure in our lives can contribute to long-term spiritual growth. Or, to be a little more theological about it, we ought to acknowledge that God can create grace in our lives even in the very midst of our suffering; or to put it in yet another way, to say that God can create good out of evil. If you find it hard to acknowledge this, pray an entire rosary without taking your eyes off the crucifix.

Today's First and Second Readings encourage us to consider Jesus' parable in the light of the Exodus of Moses and the Israelites. Saint Paul, in his first letter to the Corinthians, is very sober. He puts it plainly: even though Moses liberated all the Israelites from their slavery to the Egyptian Pharaoh, and even though all the Israelites *"ate the same spiritual food, and... drank the same spiritual drink," "God was not pleased with most of them, for they were struck down in the desert. These things happened as examples for us, so that we might not desire evil things, as they did. ... Therefore whoever thinks he is standing secure should take care not to fall."*

The sin of presumption is one of the most dangerous of all sins. We know this from our other relationships, but we often fail to recognize the presence of presumption in our spiritual life. What happens to married love when a husband takes his wife's love for granted or vice versa? What the sin of presumption does to married love, it does all the more to our love for God. In this season of Lent, Our Lord Jesus calls us to walk more closely to Him as He travels to Calvary, and to recognize how deep His love for us must be, for Him to accept death on the Cross when He has no reason to do so, save love. That is the love that God has planted within you and asks you to tend.

WEEKDAYS OF THE THIRD WEEK OF LENT

Monday of the Third Week of Lent
II Kings 5:1-15 + Luke 4:24-30

> *As the hind longs for the running waters,*
> *so my soul longs for you, O God.*

The Scriptures which the Church proclaims during Lent often paint images of water to describe our relationship with God. Many of these images come from the Psalter (the Book of Psalms). The first verse of today's Responsorial puts such an image before our mind's eye.

The deer is a gentle animal. The Bible recommends it to us often as an icon for our spiritual life. How can we imitate the deer in its gentleness and simplicity? The deer longs merely for plants and water to nourish herself. Today's Responsorial, the beginning of which comes from Psalm 42, meditates on the image of water, a metaphor for God's grace: His life and love.

As Saint Augustine says in his Confessions, man has a deep thirst for God, even if he does not recognize it. Much of human life is spent trying to quench this thirst by drinking from other streams. Yet this futility often only deepens our longing. This deepening of our longing leads either into a downward spiral, or up into an act of Faith, wherein we recognize that we must let go, and let God quench our thirst as He wills.

Tuesday of the Third Week of Lent
Daniel 3:25,34-43 + Matthew 18:21-35

"...the Kingdom of heaven may be likened to a king who decided to settle accounts with his servants."

Our Christian Faith here cuts like a two-edged sword. In the Lord's Prayer, this double edge hinges on the tiny word "as": we actually petition God to "forgive us our trespasses as we forgive those who trespass against us." The risk inherent in this double edge is the point of Jesus' parable.

Through Jesus' Passion and Death, He has offered us the Gift of re-creation, redemption, and re-conciliation. But the very nature of this Gift is such that if we do not "pay it forward", we ourselves lose the Gift.

In the face of sin and death in our own lives, then, we can choose either to act according to the logic of those who have harmed us, or according to the logic of the One who has gifted us with the Gift of Divine Mercy. We ask the Lord for the Holy Spirit's gift of Joy, to give this Gift to others not begrudgingly like Saint Peter, but with the joy of Easter Sunday.

Wednesday of the Third Week of Lent
Deuteronomy 4:1,5-9 + Matthew 5:17-19

"I have come not to abolish but to fulfill."

We want to serve the Lord faithfully, and Jesus gives us a word of encouragement today. Jesus declares in the Gospel that everything we need to know has already been revealed to us: **"Do not think that I have come to abolish the law or the prophets. I have come not to abolish but to fulfill"**. To live out our Christian Faith is to allow the fulfillment of what has already been given to us.

Blessed John Henry Cardinal Newman once said: "In a higher world it is otherwise, but here below to live is to change, and to be perfect is to have changed often" [*An Essay on the Development of Christian Doctrine* 1,1,7]. To paraphrase this saying of Newman, then: if we feel that every day we are staring into the same old face of existence, and that the world has ground to a halt, then it is surely we who have stopped moving. If we feel bored, it is because we are tired and have stopped to rest, while the world is moving on.

As we continue on the Way towards the hill of Calvary, we want to become more like Christ. We seek to give ourselves to others without measure, and this means that we imitate the fidelity of God without measure and without counting the cost. To do this is nothing more than for us to allow Christ to change us so that we share in His very life.

Thursday of the Third Week of Lent
Jeremiah 7:23-28 + Luke 11:14-23

"Every kingdom divided against itself will be laid waste and house will fall against house."

Americans can reflect on the profound examples of the Founding Fathers in establishing a human government based upon the rights and truths that come from God. Yet history shows how their efforts were met with great opposition. Their example mirrors one of the truths that Jesus makes in today's Gospel passage, summed up by the saying of Benjamin Franklin about the risks of the American Revolution: "We must all hang together, or we will all hang separately."

Unity is one of the four marks of the Church that Jesus founded when He walked this earth. Entire books have been written to explore what this mark of unity does and does not mean. Jesus' words at the end of today's Gospel passage shed some light on the matter: *"Whoever is not with me is against me, and whoever does not gather with me scatters."* The latter half of this sentence hints that the unity Jesus is calling for derives from the act of the will.

Unity—whether within the Church, within a family, within a diocese, or between an individual Christian and God—depends on individual human wills lining up with the divine Will. When human wills are in focus with the divine Will, those human wills become like a magnifying glass. The best example of a human person doing so is Mary, who begins her canticle by praying, *"My soul proclaims the greatness of the Lord"* [Luke 1:46].

Friday of the Third Week of Lent
Hosea 14:2-10 + Mark 12:28-34

"There is no other commandment greater than these."

The scribe's insight—that *"to love [the Lord] with all your heart, with all your understanding, with all your strength, and to love your neighbor as yourself is worth more than all burnt offerings and sacrifices"*—helps us understand what Jesus did for us on Mount Calvary.

First: the idea that we are to love God completely had been memorialized centuries before Jesus, in the *Shema*. But who is God? This is the question that shook the Jews' faith when Jesus declared *"I AM"*. His words were blasphemy. But revenge was had by nailing Jesus to the Cross, for they proved Jesus wrong, since God—as we all know—cannot die.

That we are to love our neighbor as ourselves was no new insight. But who is our neighbor? This is the question that shook the Jews' faith when Jesus taught the parable of the Good Samaritan. But by crucifying Jesus, they made His parables fairy tales, since Jesus could not even save Himself from death.

However, that these two insights together are *"worth more than all burnt offerings and sacrifices"* is a new insight. Every member of the human race—except Jesus and Mary—is radically estranged from God not only by our sharing in the sin of Adam, but by our personal sins as well. In the person of Jesus these two commandments become one, and in the Cross of Jesus Christ, we see the perfect Sacrifice.

Saturday of the Third Week of Lent
Hosea 6:1-6 + Luke 18:9-14

> *Then shall you be pleased with due sacrifices,*
> *burnt offerings and holocausts.*

Psalm 51 is sometimes referred to as the *"Miserere"*, which is the first word of the psalm in Latin. Psalm 51 is one of seven psalms known as the "Penitential Psalms". Not surprisingly, these seven psalms are especially interwoven through the Sacred Liturgy during the Season of Lent. Some would consider Psalm 51 to be the best known of the seven. Throughout the year, this psalm is prayed almost every Friday in the Church's *Lauds* (Morning Prayer).

In Psalm 51, there are contrasts made between the exterior sacrifices of animals, and interior subjective sacrifice. In verse 18, the Psalmist declares to God: *"you are not pleased with sacrifices; / should I offer a burnt offering, you would not accept it."* Some take these words—and similar ones elsewhere in Scripture—to mean that exterior sacrifices, such as those that Catholics practice during Lent or on Fridays throughout the year, are un-biblical.

But by the last verse of the psalm, the Psalmist sings to God that *"Then shall you be pleased with due sacrifices, / burnt offerings and holocausts."* What accounts for the change in God's consideration of exterior sacrifices? The change which is the focus of Psalm 51 is the active purification of the individual, including the purification of the desires which motivate his sacrifices. It's only through grace that the Psalmist's—and our—entreaty may come true: *"Thoroughly wash me from my guilt / and of my sin cleanse me."* When this comes true, we may and must offer fitting sacrifices of praise to God.

THE FOURTH SUNDAY OF LENT

The Fourth Sunday of Lent [A]
1 Samuel 16:1,6-7,10-13 + Ephesians 5:8-14 + John 9:1-41

*"He guides me in right paths
for his name's sake."*

The Fourth Sunday of Easter is popularly called "Good Shepherd Sunday". Every year on that Sunday the Gospel passage is taken from the tenth chapter of St. John's Gospel account, where Jesus describes Himself at length as *"the good shepherd"* and even as *"the gate for the sheep"*. But today, on this Fourth Sunday of Lent, we also hear about the Good Shepherd, though from the Old Testament rather than the New. Today's Responsorial Psalm is the most beloved song of the Psalter: the 23rd Psalm.

At first hearing, it might not seem that this psalm connects with the other three Scripture passages proclaimed today. True, in today's First Reading, the young man David is described as *"tending the sheep"*, and is plucked from this role to be anointed the king—that is, the shepherd—of God's People. But for the most part, today's Scripture passages focus on another theme: blindness.

Nonetheless, we should never underestimate the depth of Sacred Scripture. If we look closely, we might be able to see a connection between these two Lenten themes. Today's First Reading is a good place to start looking for a connection between these themes of Our Lord as Shepherd, and ourselves as blind sinners. In fact, the First Reading focuses on both themes. Yet the conclusion of this passage is the anointing of young David as the king of Israel, so surely this theme of the shepherd/king is the passage's chief point?

Well, consider something that happens earlier in the passage. Samuel seeks the LORD's anointed from among the sons of Jesse, and he does find him, but it takes eight tries to do so. What is it that hinders Samuel's search? It is his faulty sight.

Samuel judges wrongly because he is blind to the truth of what God's shepherd looks like. The LORD explains this to Samuel as plainly as possible, saying: *"Not as man sees does God see, because man sees the appearance but the LORD looks into the heart."* This blindness that the LORD exposes lies at the root of all our sins. This blindness can take many forms. But the LORD here is not just condemning the shallow outlook so common today, which believes that beauty is only skin deep and that only what our senses perceive truly exists.

The LORD here in our First Reading is condemning something more specific: the blindness that keeps us from seeing our shepherd. Samuel judges wrongly because he sees only the appearance, and looks for a man's lofty stature instead of looking into his heart. But this blindness takes on an even more tragic form in today's Gospel passage.

The Pharisees bear a double blindness. Not only are they spiritually blind, but they are also blind to the fact of their blindness. At least the man born blind knew he was blind! Yet the Pharisees, blind to their blindness, attempt to lead others spiritually in their zeal for the Jewish Law. In Matthew's Gospel account, Jesus is direct in calling the Pharisees *"blind guides"*, and notes that *"if a blind man leads a blind man, both will fall into a pit"* [Matthew 15:14].

The Pharisees' double blindness is spiritually a *"dark valley"*. They walk through it without a capable guide. Their zeal for the Law stems from the blindness that the LORD pointed out to Samuel: they look at the appearances of legal observance. Their blindness prevents them from seeing Jesus as Lord and Shepherd: as one who *"looks into the heart"*.

But as you and I reflect on these blind guides, we each need to ask two questions. First, am I blind like the Pharisees? Second, what hope is there for someone suffering from such a double blindness? The answer to the second can help us honestly answer the first.

The spiritually blind person has no reason for hope in himself. Hope for the spiritually blind rests in God alone. Their hope—our hope—rests in the truth that our LORD is a Good Shepherd. The Good Shepherd *"looks into the heart"*, and sees only darkness there. But He wills to lead the blind from darkness into light.

The Pharisees can see into neither their own blind hearts nor the heart of Jesus. But Jesus sees into the Pharisees' hearts, and seeing their blindness, will on Good Friday pour forth from His Sacred Heart the light of Divine Mercy. But will the Pharisees turn toward His light, or avert their gaze from Him?

The Fourth Sunday of Lent [B]
II Chronicles 36:14-16,19-23 + Ephesians 2:4-10 + John 3:14-21

But whoever lives the truth comes to the light....

In today's Gospel passage, St. John is not commenting on the light in the sky. He's not talking about the light that shines brighter and longer in the evening once our clocks "spring forward". St. John is describing something both moral and spiritual.

On the one hand, St. John describes moral choices in terms of light or darkness. He states that *"everyone who does wicked things hates the light and does not come toward the light.... But whoever lives the truth comes to the light...."* In the moral life, light symbolizes truth. In common speech, when we say that someone fears his actions "coming to light", we mean that someone fears the truth of his actions becoming known. Along this line, St. John explains how one person *"does not come toward the light"* so that his action will not become known. Then there's the person who *"comes to the light, so that his works may be clearly seen"*.

On the other hand, St. John describes spiritual choices, and what he says here goes further. Saint John in his first epistle proclaims the truth that *"God is light"*. Likewise, it's St. John who reveals the truth that Jesus is *"the light of the world"*. Nowhere in the Gospel account of Matthew, or Mark, or Luke, does Jesus call Himself *"light"*, but only in *John*, where Jesus calls Himself *"light"* three times.

St. John is revealing to us that God, by His very nature, enlightens by showing the truth: that is, by showing us Himself. This is so important a spiritual truth that St. John foreshadows this in the prologue to his Gospel account: the first eighteen verses of the Gospel account. There, John proclaims that *"The true light, which enlightens everyone, was coming into the world. He was in the world, and the world came to be through him, but the world did not know him"* [John 1:9-10].

Relate this, then, to what St. John saw as he stood fast at the foot of the Cross. To the Romans, Jesus' crucifixion was punishment for threatening their rule. To the Jews, Jesus' crucifixion was justice for a man who claimed to be their Messiah. But the Beloved Disciple saw infinitely more: to St. John, Jesus' crucifixion was a two-fold icon. Just as Jesus is truly human and truly divine, so the icon of Jesus' crucifixion is two-fold. To St. John, Jesus' crucifixion is the icon of God's love for him, and the icon of St. John's own vocation as a beloved disciple.

The icon of the crucifixion reveals the measure of God's love for man, and in this, reveals God's measure for how man is called to love. The two are one in the Sacrifice of Jesus. Each of us, as a member of the Body that Jesus sacrificed on Calvary, is called to accept Jesus' sacrifice as one's own.

In terms of your own spiritual life, consider that whenever you look at the state of your moral life—say, during night prayers in looking back over the day's choices; or, kneeling in a pew, preparing for the Sacrament of Confession; or, in reflection during a mission or retreat—you need a measuring stick. This is important for effectively assessing your moral life. You can purchase different pamphlets or booklets to help you make an examination of conscience. Each may employ a measuring stick different from the rest: one the Ten Commandments, another the Beatitudes, another the cardinal and theological virtues. Each of these can be effective.

But in the end, God uses only two measuring sticks. The first is the vertical beam of the Cross, that stretches from earth to Heaven: that is the command to love one's God. The second is the horizontal beam of the Cross, against which the hands of Jesus were nailed: that is the command to love one's neighbor.

There is no better place to spend your life than at the feet of Jesus, in the company of Our Blessed Mother and the Beloved Disciple. As Jesus hangs from the Cross, it's in your gazing upon His self-sacrifice that you can grow in your resolve to stand fast with Him. There, you can accept Jesus for the light that He is: God's infinite love for you, which allows you not only to be forgiven, but also to be transparent in sharing that same forgiveness with others, including most especially those who offend you the greatest.

The Fourth Sunday of Lent [C]
Joshua 5:9,10-12 + 2 Corinthians 5:17-21 + Luke 15:1-3,11-32

He ran to his son, embraced him and kissed him.

Jesus' parable of the Prodigal Son is one of the more touching of our Savior's teachings. Jesus clearly paints for us a picture of His heavenly Father, and reveals to us how deep the Father's compassion is. We might say that the parable of the Prodigal Son is to the Gospel what the 23rd Psalm is to the Book of Psalms.

The father's compassion in the parable is revealed, of course, precisely because of the infidelity of his two sons. This is worth pondering. In other words, if the sons didn't behave so poorly, we would never see the father's compassion. That's part of the paradox of forgiveness and compassion: we'd rather never have to receive them, because forgiveness and compassion exist only where there is sin and suffering in our lives. But when I have sinned and am suffering because of the fallout from my sins, I definitely want to receive forgiveness and compassion.

The Church proclaims this paradox—this mystery—every year at the Easter Vigil. Even if the Sacraments of Initiation are not conferred during the Mass, the Easter Vigil still begins with the lighting of the Easter Candle either outdoors or in the vestibule. Then the Easter Candle is carried in procession to the sanctuary. Once the procession reaches the sanctuary, the *Exultet* is either chanted or spoken. The *Exultet* is the greatest chant of the Church. It's been sung since the first centuries of the Church's history. In the midst of the *Exultet*, the Church proclaims these words: *"O wonder of your humble care for us! / O love, O charity beyond all telling, / to ransom a slave you gave away your Son! / O truly necessary sin of Adam, / destroyed completely by the Death of Christ! / O happy fault / that earned so great, so glorious a Redeemer!"*

Just how a "fault" can be "happy" is something that we can only understand by meditating upon the crucifix. Adam's sin was "necessary" in the sense that, if Adam had not brought sin into the world, then Christ never would have had to die on the

Cross, and so we would not have had revealed to us just how deep God's love for us must be.

It's as if Christ, our brother, is the opposite of the older brother in the parable of the Prodigal Son. Jesus Christ, the first-born of all creation, is our older brother who not only rejoices in the forgiveness shown his younger brother. Jesus chose to do far more than just rejoice: He chose to descend from His rightful place, to give up His own inheritance as the Only-Begotten Son of the Father, so that we who are not God's children by nature, could be adopted by the Father through the sacrifice of the true Son. Jesus took on our human nature, and through His humanity, by sacrificing Himself completely—His Body and Blood, soul and divinity—He became the reason why we have the chance to receive compassion, forgiveness, and eternal life.

We can meditate on Jesus' parable of the Prodigal Son in twenty different ways and then some. We can apply this parable to our daily life by putting ourselves in the shoes of the prodigal, the younger sibling. Certainly, during the season of Lent, as we do penance, and approach God through sacramental confession, recognizing our *"dire need"* for God's grace, and *"coming to [our] senses, [we] get up and go to [our] father and... say to him, 'Father, I have sinned against heaven and against you. I no longer deserve to be called your son....'"* But God our Father replies to us by proclaiming to everyone, *"'let us celebrate with a feast, because this son of mine was dead, and has come to life again; he was lost, and has been found.'"* We celebrate this feast at Easter and, in fact, every Sunday, each Sunday being a "little Easter".

Put yourself in the shoes of the Prodigal Father: prodigal because there's no length that He won't go to—in fact, run to—in order to bring His children back into His embrace. If you find yourself unable to be as generous as the Father, then you are the elder brother of today's parable, and need to turn to the Father for that love, mercy and compassion that He is simply waiting to shower upon you.

WEEKDAYS OF THE FOURTH WEEK OF LENT

Monday of the Fourth Week of Lent
Isaiah 65:17-21 + John 4:43-54

Lo, I am about to create new heavens
and a new earth....

In the First Reading, Isaiah reminds us that what we are preparing for during Lent is something unprecedented. *"Lo, I am about to create new heavens / and a new earth...."* Lent prepares us for what the Church celebrates during the "Sacred Triduum". Through the mysteries of these three days, the LORD creates a new heavens and a new earth.

In today's Gospel, St. John the Evangelist hints at what Jesus is preparing to do for us during the Sacred Triduum, and why He would do so. The last verse of the Gospel passage tells us that the event in this passage was the *"second sign"*. Throughout the second to twelfth chapters of *John*, the evangelist records seven signs that Jesus works. Each of these seven prepares us for the Sacred Triduum.

To reflect on today's *"second sign"*, listen closely to the royal official's request: what exactly does he ask for? He asks Jesus to *"come down and heal his son."* Reflect upon his petitions in terms of how you petition God. Does Jesus grant the official's request? No and yes. Jesus does not *"come down"* as He had been requested to do. So the official repeats his request: *"Sir, come down before my child dies."* Jesus again does not *"come down"*. Nor does He need to. Instead, He simply says, *"You may go; your son will live."* This teaches us about our expectations of Jesus, and that He does not need our expectations.

Tuesday of the Fourth Week of Lent
Ezekiel 47:1-9,12 + John 5:1-16

Then he brought me to the bank of the river, where he had me sit.

Today's Gospel passage narrates the "third sign" of John's account. Each of these seven signs from John 2-12 bring us closer to Jesus' Passion, Death and Resurrection.

This third sign is like the second in that Jesus demonstrates the immediacy of His divine power. The ill man explains that he has not been cured because he cannot reach the healing waters. But Jesus does not help the man into the waters. He does not even explain that the waters are unnecessary for the man's healing. Jesus simply says, **"Rise, take up your mat, and walk."**

This third sign is a turning point in John's Gospel account. The last sentence of the passage ominously tells us that it was because of this sign that **"the Jews began to persecute Jesus because he did this on a sabbath."**

The First Reading today, from *Ezekiel*, foreshadows the power of Christ on Calvary. The Jewish Temple often foreshadows Christ Himself (**"in him dwells the whole fullness of the deity bodily"** [Colossians 2:9]), or the Church as the Body of Christ, or Heaven. But in Ezekiel 47 the focus is not so much the Temple itself as it is the water that flows abundantly from the Temple. In these words the Church prepares us for Good Friday and the water pouring from Christ's side, that water in turn symbolizing the healing waters of Baptism.

Wednesday of the Fourth Week of Lent
Isaiah 49:8-15 + John 5:17-30

"My Father is at work until now, so I am at work."

In the accounts of the Gospel—especially in *Matthew* and *John*—Jesus often, after working a miracle, teaches at length.

Following the miracle—the sign—that we yesterday heard Jesus perform, today's Gospel passage is the beginning of a larger teaching discourse which makes us the remainder of John 5. What is Jesus teaching us here? The first two verses set up further conflict between Jesus and the Jewish officials. Through the rest of the passage, Jesus explores his claims as a worker of signs, and this, in terms of His relationship with God the Father.

In the first two verses of today's Gospel passage, Jesus compounds the conflict between Himself and the Jewish officials beyond His having broken the sabbath by calling God His Father in today's Gospel passage, in effect *"making himself equal to God."*

Here is one of the most important themes of John's Gospel account: the divinity of Jesus Christ. The prologue of John [John 1:1-18] illustrates this theme poetically. Today's Gospel passage illustrates the same theme prosaically through Jesus' own words.

One way of describing your own spiritual life as a Christian disciple is to say that your spiritual life is a journey into the relationship of God the Father and God the Son: a journey into the relationship of God the Father and God the Son. This may seem like an abstract claim. In fact, it is profoundly personal. You grow as a Christian—and indeed, as a person—inasmuch as you grow into this relationship of the Father and the Son with each other. Reflect upon today's Gospel passage with this in mind: that it has something to reveal to you about the authentic path of your inner, spiritual life.

Thursday of the Fourth Week of Lent
Exodus 32:7-14 + John 5:31-47

"But I have testimony greater than John's."

Jesus mentions a number of "witnesses" that He has: John the Baptist; the works that the Father gave Him; *"the Father who sent me"*; and the Scriptures. But what do these witness to about Jesus: that He ran a red light? that's He's a nice guy? that He's the son of Mary? Jesus explains, in speaking about the witness of His works: **"these works that I perform testify on my behalf that the Father has sent me."**

If you were to ask the average Christian, "Why did Jesus die on the Cross?", you might hear, "To wash away our sins." This is true. But Jesus' Passion, Death and Resurrection accomplish more than this only. The Cross and Resurrection are the foundation of one's Christian life.

The phrase "one's Christian life" sounds a little abstract, but at the foundation of the Christian life is the truth that through Jesus Christ, we are sons and daughters of God the Father. There is nothing abstract about this relationship. The glory of the Resurrection is a glory that is promised to us as God's sons and daughters. But what is most moving about this truth is that we already share in this glory, if but dimly, to the extent that we live our Christian life now as witnesses to Jesus Christ, the Father's only-begotten Son.

Friday of the Fourth Week of Lent
Wisdom 2:1,12-22 + John 7:1-2,10,25-30

...but no one laid a hand upon him, because his hour had not yet come.

Today's First Reading, from the Old Testament *Book of Wisdom*, sounds as if it could have been written by one of the four evangelists, recording his Passion narrative. The First Reading seems exactly what those who plotted Jesus' death would have said as they explained to themselves their rationale for His crucifixion.

One way, then, to reflect on today's First Reading is to apply it as a salve against any persecution that you yourself may have faced (or face today) because of standing for the Truth who is Christ. Especially comforting is the final sentence, in which the biblical author offers commentary against the thoughts of the wicked.

However, during Lent it would be more fitting to take a different tack to this First Reading. Read through the words of the wicked as a sort of Examination of Conscience. Gossip, calumny and slander are sins that most Christians participate in either directly or indirectly. These three sins, and others related to them, are common enough to cause great harm to the Body of Christ, especially to families and to fellow parishioners. Reflecting on the First Reading, ask whether your any of your relationships with others, or even your opinions of them, demand purification.

Saturday of the Fourth Week of Lent
Jeremiah 11:18-20 + John 7:40-53

> *"...let us cut him off from the land of the living,*
> *so that his name will be spoken no more."*

Of the four major Old Testament prophets, Isaiah tends to be associated with the Season of Advent, and Jeremiah with Lent. No prophet has an easy life, but if we were to define the prophet by hardships leveled against him, Jeremiah would be the prophet *par excellence*.

This relates to us, because through the Sacrament of Baptism, the Christian is called to live out three roles: priest, prophet, and king. If we reflect fruitfully on Jeremiah's life as a prophet, then, we can live our Christian life better, if not comfortably.

The hardships that Jeremiah faces in today's First Reading deal with what we might call either his "reputation" or "worldly honor". Such honor—the honor of esteem of one's neighbors—is an earthly good that many people go to great lengths to protect. St. Thomas Aquinas cites such honor as one of the goods in which fallen man falsely seeks happiness. The Angelic Doctor notes that seeking happiness in one's reputation is putting the cart before the horse: St. Thomas explains that authentic "honor is given to a man on account of some excellence in him.... Now a man's excellence is in proportion, especially to his happiness, which is man's perfect good.... And therefore honor can result from happiness, but happiness cannot principally consist therein." [*Summa Theologica*, II-I,2,2 *sed contra*].

So when the good of one's honor is placed above God, a disorder is created. Jeremiah willingly suffered calumny and many other attacks against his name (which symbolically represents one's honor) because of his fidelity to God's prophetic message. Recall the last of Jesus' Beatitudes as recorded by St. Luke, and pray for such blessedness in your own spiritual life: *"Blessed are you when people hate you.... / Behold, your reward / will be great in heaven. / For their ancestors treated the prophets / in the same way"* [Luke 6:22,23].

THE FIFTH SUNDAY OF LENT

The Fifth Sunday of Lent [A]
Ezekiel 37:12-14 + Romans 8:8-11 + John 11:1-45

"'...whoever believes in me, even if he dies, will live....'"

For whose benefit did Jesus raise Lazarus from the dead? What did Lazarus himself gain? Wasn't he better off—a step closer to Heaven—after leaving this world? From all that we are and are not told by the Scriptures, we gather that Jesus brought Lazarus back to the same sort of life that he had previously had. Presumably Lazarus died a second time some years later. So what did Lazarus get out of being brought back to life, except for a few more years in this vale of tears?

Did Jesus raise Lazarus from the dead for the sake of Martha and Mary? Certainly they were overjoyed to see their brother alive again. They were blessed not only emotionally, but also practically. In the first century, they—as women—would have depended largely on their brother for their sustenance. So was Jesus simply "playing favorites" on behalf of two close friends?

Why, during the three years of His public ministry, didn't Jesus raise many others from the dead? Certainly in the first century adults had a much lower life expectancy than today, and infant mortality was very high. Why didn't Jesus focus His divine power on raising all those persons from the dead? Was Jesus showing preferential treatment, or is there something more to His miracle?

There is something more. But to see it, and be better prepared for Holy Week, we have to see the bigger picture of St. John the Evangelist's account of the Gospel.

Just as the entire Bible is divided into the Old and New Testaments, so St. John's Gospel account is divided into two parts. St. John himself didn't give titles to these two halves, but in modern times they are called "The Book of Signs" and "The Book of Glory". Just as the Old Testament is full of signs that foreshadow the Messiah who is to come, so the first half of St. John's Gospel account is full of signs that foreshadow the glory revealed in the second half. In fact, "The Book of Signs" in St. John's Gospel account has exactly seven signs. St. John specifically calls them "signs" as he builds up to the events of Holy Week.

The seven signs that St. John the Evangelist records are very different from each other. The first of them occurs at the wedding at Cana. Jesus turns water into wine: certainly a miracle, but certainly not a matter of life or death. In fact, compared to the raising of Lazarus from the dead, this first miracle seems almost trivial. But that's part of John's point. He is building to a crescendo as he narrates "The Book of Signs", and the raising of Lazarus is the final sign. It's the sign that most clearly points to the glory that it foreshadows.

Jesus worked this miracle to reveal as unmistakably as possible who He is and what power He has: the divine Son of God who can raise the dead to life because He is the Creator of life. Jesus also raised Lazarus for the sake of you, who are a sinner. Jesus worked this miracle in order to draw all sinners to Himself.

Of course, there's an important difference between this final sign and the glory it foreshadows. To reflect on this difference, consider the Latin adage: *"Nemo dat quod non habet"*, meaning "No one gives what he doesn't have." Jesus could not have transformed water into wine unless He "had it within Him" to so. Likewise, Jesus could not have raised Lazarus from the dead unless He had that power within Him. Jesus as a divine Person had and has power over all creation, including human life.

However, what about at the end of Good Friday? After Jesus expired on the Cross, what did Jesus have? In the view of His enemies, He was nothing. He was finished. Jesus after His death could give nothing and do nothing, because He had nothing. But they were wrong.

Jesus' death at 3:00 in the afternoon on Good Friday was His finest hour. It shows most clearly who He is. It shows that from His Cross He reigns as Christ the King. Jesus from within death displays the depth of the power that He has over death.

On Easter Sunday morning, God the Father did not raise the corpse of Jesus to life as Jesus raised Lazarus' corpse to life. The *Catechism of the Catholic Church* explains that God the Son "effects His own Resurrection by virtue of His divine power" [649]. The Catechism then links this assertion to the Lord's own words: *"I lay down my life in order to take it up again. ... I have power to lay it down, and power to take it up again"* [John 10:17,18]. Jesus spoke these words in the chapter before the one from which today's Gospel passage comes.

At the Liturgy of the Lord's Passion on Good Friday, why do we kiss the corpus of Jesus? This action is not only a sad, tender act of gratitude. Nor is it only a heartfelt act of contrition. It is an act of adoration, worshipping not the wooden corpus itself, but the Savior beyond our sight who through His very death holds the power to destroy our sins.

The Fifth Sunday of Lent [B]
Jeremiah 31:31-34 + Hebrews 5:7-9 + John 12:20-33

"But it was for this purpose that I came to this hour."

The Resurrection of Jesus is a sign of hope for us, not only because it means that God is more powerful than death, and not only because it means that we have a chance to enter Heaven. The Resurrection of Jesus is also a sign, a foreshadowing, of what will happen to each one of us if we believe in Christ Crucified. When your life is over on this earth, God will make a particular judgment of your life, and your soul will go to either Hell or Heaven. If, of course, you have accepted God in faith but have not been completely purified of worldly desires, your journey towards Heaven will take you through Purgatory, so that you would be purified of any sin and temporal punishment.

However, at the end of time when Christ comes to the earth a second time, there will be another judgment: a general judgment. This is the judgment that Jesus describes as the separation of the sheep from the goats. This is the belief that we profess when we recite the Creed and say that Christ *"will come again in glory / to judge the living and the dead"*.

Nonetheless, on this fifth Sunday of Lent, as we hear again a passage from Saint John's Gospel account, Jesus presents us with His last teaching before we enter into Holy Week next Sunday. The heart of Jesus' teaching is simple: *"unless a grain of wheat falls to the ground and dies, it remains just a grain of wheat; but if it dies, it produces much fruit."* Obviously, this passage refers both to Jesus and to us.

The end of today's Gospel passage says plainly that these words of Jesus indicated the sort of death He was going to die. That death would be followed by His Resurrection. We could even say that His Death was the cause of His Resurrection. But Jesus' resurrection was not the only fruit of His Death: after all, if the grain of wheat falls to the earth and dies, it produces much fruit. The resurrection of each person who has faith in the power of Jesus' Death is also a fruit of His Death. We hope that our own resurrection at the Second Coming is such fruit.

But if we imagine ourselves at the end of time, at the Final Judgment, hopefully we would be expecting to see everyone judged worthy to enter Heaven. Hopefully each of us would, in a sense, be cheering for every other human person as he or she was judged.

From a human point of view, I think we would find the Final Judgment more difficult to undergo than our particular judgment at the moment of death. That particular judgment, before God, is swift and sure: after all, God already knows everything there is to know about us, including things we might try to forget.

But at the Final Judgment, all mankind is present, even the members of our own families. As we imagine our parents, our siblings, and our co-workers watching every detail and every sin of our lives, even those we did manage to hide from them, we would realize just how many people's lives our actions, and inactions, affect. If we refuse to die to our selves—if we fail to develop the virtue of humility as the basis of our faith—then we will bear little fruit.

Even more serious, however, is the honest fact—which will be revealed at the Final Judgment—that our actions or inactions not only may bear little fruit in our lives, but may also keep others from bearing fruit in their lives. If we find it awkward to watch our lives reviewed at the Final Judgment, we'll likely find it even more difficult to watch the lives of those we know reviewed: those whom we failed to help carry their crosses, and who bore consequences in their spiritual lives because of our failure to be with them when they needed someone to bring God's strength and compassion to them.

Perhaps we would like to downplay the idea that our lives are really bound up with the lives of others. In John's account of Jesus' teaching that is proclaimed today, it's no coincidence that it is Greeks—that is, foreigners—who approach Jesus, and that it is only through others—in this case, through the apostles Philip and Andrew—that these foreigners are able to hear Jesus teach the very heart of the Gospel: *"unless a grain of wheat falls to the ground and dies, it remains just a grain of wheat; but if it dies, it produces much fruit."*

The Fifth Sunday of Lent [C]
Isaiah 43:16-21 + Philippians 3:8-14 + John 8:1-11

It is not that I have already taken hold of it or have already attained perfect maturity....

As we continue to journey through the season of Lent, we are journeying along the way of the Cross. This way leads to Jerusalem and the hill of Calvary, where we will face our Maker and Redeemer as He hangs upon the Cross. Unfortunately, the road that leads to Calvary takes us over rocky ground. Oftentimes we find ourselves in life between a rock and a hard place. Drawing grace from Jesus, we can find ourselves locked between standing up for the truth and facing what seems a form of death.

In everyday life, our own sins and the sins of others often cloud our sight and keep us from seeing the big picture. The scribes and the Pharisees in today's Gospel passage are trying to form a cloud like this over Jesus and the woman caught in sin. As we meditate on this passage, we might first imagine ourselves to be the Pharisees, and then secondly the woman caught in sin.

Looking at the confrontation between Jesus and the Pharisees, they were trying to put Jesus between a rock and a hard place. Here was Jesus, this supposedly learned and wise rabbi or teacher of the law. Jesus certainly knew that the Law of Moses proscribed death for anyone caught in the act of adultery. Yet there's another important fact that today's Gospel passage does not explain. The Pharisees knew that Roman law, which overruled Jewish law since the Romans controlled the land of Jewish people, had forbidden the Jewish people from carrying out any death penalty: to do so was considered insurrection against the authority of the Caesar. So was Jesus to insist that this woman caught in sin be stoned, and face a Roman charge of insurrection; or was he to insist that she should not be stoned, and thereby prove himself a hypocrite regarding Jewish teaching, which was exactly what Jesus had been accusing the Pharisees of being?

When Jesus says, *"Let the one among you who is without sin be the first to throw a stone at her"*, the crowd began to drift away. They did so not simply because they realized that they, too, were sinners. The Pharisees, like Saint Paul before his conversion, held themselves to be completely upstanding before the Law, with not a single sin on their conscience. Indeed, to walk away at this point would be to admit their own hypocrisy. Yet this is exactly what they were forced to do by Jesus, because each was unwilling to throw the first stone and expose himself to the charge of insurrection from the Romans. Once again Jesus had forced the Pharisees to show their true colors. This is why this experience simply fueled their anger against Jesus.

At this point, then, the confrontation would seem to be over. The final words exchanged between Jesus and the adulterous woman seem simply to wrap up the story. Yet in these last words we see the heart of the Gospel revealed to us. So we need to reflect on ourselves as this woman, caught in mortal sin.

For the Pharisees, this woman was no more than a pawn to be pushed across a chessboard, to trap Jesus into a position of checkmate. But now Jesus had cleared the board of everyone except Himself and this woman. The manner in which He treats her is the same manner that He treats each of us in our relationship with Him, and is the same manner in which we are called to deal with our own brothers and sisters.

At first glance, it could seem that Jesus' refusal to condemn the woman means that He approved of her actions, or at least that her actions were not something to worried about. However, in sending her forth, Jesus tells her that what she has done is indeed a sin, one which she must avoid in the future.

But Jesus refuses to condemn her in the midst of her life. To put it somewhat flippantly, condemnation is sending someone to Hell before his time. Certainly this woman's sin is something that deserves eternal punishment, but Jesus refuses to equate the woman with her sin. It is not sin alone which condemns a person to eternal punishment: a person must also persist in holding onto that sin, refusing to see it as sinful and/or refusing to turn towards God for His merciful forgiveness. The Lord will not let even mortal sin—as an infinite offense against His love—stand in the way of our sharing in His love. As long as a person still has a moment to live on this earth, he still has the chance to recognize his sinfulness, to turn to God in sorrow, and to ask for mercy. This season of Lent is the time to let go of our sins, to make sure that they do not define us, and to accept God's gift of mercy and its power to make us better than our sins.

WEEKDAYS OF THE FIFTH WEEK OF LENT

Monday of the Fifth Week of Lent
Daniel 13:41-62 + John 8:1-11

"'Let the one among you who is without sin be the first to throw a stone at her.'"

After the crowd shows their unwillingness to stone the adulterous woman, today's Gospel scene might seem over. The final words exchanged in the Gospel between Jesus and her would seem to be simply a wrapping up of the story. Yet in these last words, we see the heart of the Gospel revealed to us. We should see ourselves as this woman.

At first glance, it could seem that Jesus' refusal to condemn the woman means that He approved of her actions, or at least that her actions were not something to worried about. However, in sending her forth, Jesus tells her that what she has done is indeed a sin, one which she must avoid in the future.

Jesus refuses to condemn her in the midst of her life. To put it somewhat flippantly, condemning another human being is sending someone to Hell before his time. Certainly the woman's sin is something that deserves eternal punishment, but Jesus refuses to equate the woman and her sin. It is not sin alone which condemns a person to eternal punishment: a person must also persist in holding onto that sin, refusing to see it as sinful, and refusing to embrace God's grace instead of sin. As long as a person still has a day to live on this earth—even a moment—he still has the chance to recognize his sinfulness, to turn to God in sorrow, and to ask for mercy.

Tuesday of the Fifth Week of Lent
Numbers 21:4-9 + John 8:21-30

...whenever anyone who had been bitten by a serpent looked at the bronze serpent, he lived.

Today's First Reading is proclaimed each year on September 14, the Feast of the Exaltation of the Holy Cross. This passage from Numbers, then, setting before us the Israelites in their sinfulness during the Exodus, foreshadows us as sinners during Lent.

The pole on which Moses mounts the bronze serpent foreshadows the Cross. More importantly, the bronze serpent foreshadows Jesus crucified. This latter connection might seem hard to grasp, or even cruel to say regarding our Savior. But we need to remember what St. Paul teaches us about Jesus in his second letter to the Corinthians, as we heard at Holy Mass on Ash Wednesday: *"For our sake [the Father] made him to be sin who did not know sin, so that we might become the righteousness of God in him"* [2 Corinthians 5:21].

However, in every Old Testament foreshadowing of the New, there is something vital lacking. Here, *"the children of Israel"* recognize that it's because of their sins that serpents bit many, bringing death. The bronze serpent brings healing to them, but does not take away their sins, or rescue those who have already died. In this, the bronze serpent brings only further life in this world. It does not, as Christ crucified does, bring forgiveness of sins, resurrection from the death of mortal sin, or life in the world to come.

Wednesday of the Fifth Week of Lent
Daniel 3:14-20,91-92,95 + John 8:31-42

"If you remain in my word, you will truly be my disciples, and you will know the truth, and the truth will set you free."

The truth that Jesus speaks about here is Jesus Himself. Elsewhere in St. John's Gospel account, He says of Himself: *"I am the way and the truth and the life."* But this truth is so powerful—its light is so bright—that it shines everywhere, including upon the lives of us poor sinners.

Sinners flee from the truth, because the light of truth exposes their sins for what they are. But if we could only offer our sins to Jesus, He would take them upon Himself, and we could approach the Truth who is Jesus in purity of heart.

Remember what will happen upon Mount Calvary next Friday. From the Cross, Jesus will silently defend a guilty human race from a just punishment: the punishment of eternal damnation. He will defend us by taking our place, and by offering His Body and Blood, soul and divinity, for the forgiveness of all mankind. He will become sin, so that from within, he might transform sin and death through the power of divine love.

When you see an image of the Sacred Heart, you see an antidote for the culture that surrounds us. Jesus points only to Himself, to the innocent Lamb who was slain. He points to His own Sacred Heart. He invites us—most especially through the Eucharistic Sacrifice of Holy Mass—to enter into this love: a love which shows mercy to the guilty, and forgiveness to those without hope.

Thursday of the Fifth Week of Lent
Genesis 17:3-9 + John 8:51-59

Jesus said to them, "Amen, amen, I say to you, before Abraham came to be, I AM."

Many Scriptural studies in recent years have focused on the notion of "covenant" as a key to interpreting the whole of the Bible. Throughout the Old Testament, the Lord makes covenants with several figures, including Abram. In today's First Reading God changes Abram's name to "Abraham" as a reflection of their covenant.

The name "Abraham" literally signifies that God is making him *"the father of a host of nations"*. Their covenant also concerns *"the whole land of Canaan"* which the Lord gives *"as a permanent possession"* of that *"host of nations"*. The Lord promises to maintain this covenant *"throughout the ages as an everlasting pact"*. Yet for their part, Abraham and his descendants also must keep the Lord's *"covenant throughout the ages."*

We might ask how Jesus would have thought of this covenant in light of His own mission. At the beginning of today's Gospel passage, *"Jesus said to the Jews: '...whoever keeps my word will never see death."* Interpret these words in light of the Lord's covenant with Abraham. Abraham's name signifies his endurance through his progeny. Yet in the Christian's covenant with Jesus, it's not one's progeny but oneself who perdures by never seeing death.

Friday of the Fifth Week of Lent
Jeremiah 20:10-13 + John 10:31-42

"You, a man, are making yourself God."

It was the humble, ordinary citizens with little to lose who by simple faith and "common sense" accepted Jesus. John the Baptist's witness, coupled with Christ's many signs and wonders, convinced them of the truth of Jesus' claims.

Humility is the single most important attribute in opening human hearts and minds to God. We receive from God to the degree that we relinquish our very selves.

It is ironic that the Pharisees' argument against Jesus is the following: *"You, a man, are making yourself God."* This lies at the root of the charges that will lead Jesus to His Passion and Death. It is not, of course, Jesus who "made" Himself God: rather, from eternity, God the Son was begotten by the Father. This same Father gave Jesus His mission in this world. In rejecting both who Jesus is, and His mission, the Pharisees reject

God the Father as well.

Adding to the irony of the Pharisees' charge is that human sin—whose power God the Son came into this world to destroy—is based precisely on what they charge Jesus with doing: making oneself into a god. From Adam and Eve to your own sins, every human sinner makes himself an arbiter of truth, and of the meaning of life. Instead, God calls each of us to turn humbly to the Father each day.

Saturday of the Fifth Week of Lent
Ezekiel 37:21-28 + John 11:45-56

...he prophesied that Jesus was going to die for the nation....

In today's Gospel passage, the chief priests and Pharisees worry about how Jesus might hurt their standing. They say, *"'What are we going to do? This man is performing many signs.'"*

Their chief complaint about Jesus is that He's able to perform signs that threaten them. The ironic point is that in this, the chief priests and Pharisees are like most of the crowds who watch and listen to Jesus. The crowds, in large measure, follow Jesus because of the signs He performs.

Both His enemies and His followers see Jesus' signs in relation to themselves. His enemies see His signs as leading to their losing power. His followers see His signs as leading to their gaining food and healing.

Yet neither group considers what the signs are pointing to. For this reason, it's easy to see why, atop Calvary on Good Friday, His followers are not to be found, and His enemies jeer that His signs have come to an end. *"'Let the Christ, the King of Israel, come down now from the cross that we may see and believe'"* [Mark 15:31-32]. Here is a further irony: both friend and foe fail to see the power of the Sign of the Cross. The Cross bears the power to bring strength to His enemies in the form of forgiveness, and nourishment and healing of soul to those who will follow Him in taking up their own crosses.

PALM SUNDAY
OF THE PASSION OF THE LORD

Palm Sunday of the Passion of the Lord [A]
Isaiah 50:4-7 + Philippians 2:6-11 + Matthew 26:14—27:66

Rather, he emptied himself
taking the form of a slave....

In the year 30 A.D., Jesus of Nazareth found His Name being shouted loudly. Today, in the twenty-first century, we join in the shouting. The question, though, is what we shout along with His name: as we cry the name of Jesus Christ, are we crying "Hosanna to Jesus!", or are we crying "Crucify Jesus!"?

This question—this two-edged sword—is why this day has two names: Palm Sunday and Passion Sunday. Most of us tend to prefer the name Palm Sunday, but in the second Gospel passage of today's Mass, the congregation proclaims the Passion of Jesus' death, and participate in that Passion. We within that congregation participate in the sufferings of Jesus, just as we throughout the year by means of our daily sacrifices. Each Christian is a member of Christ's Body. So in all that you do, you either bring glory to Christ's Body, or you crucify it. In every decision of right or wrong that you make, you shout as those two groups shouted 2000 years ago.

On the one side of the sword, there is the crowd that laid their cloaks before Jesus on the path leading into Jerusalem. The other side of the sword—which pierced Jesus' own side—is the crowd mocking Jesus as he carried the Cross on the path up to Calvary. At the top of Calvary were the soldiers who placed a military cloak upon Jesus, mocking the claim that He was the King of the Jews.

The sharpest cut that this two-edged sword makes is the fact that these two crowds were—for the most part—made up of the same people. In the year 30 A.D., it was largely the same people on Sunday shouting "Hosanna to Jesus!" who five days later were shouting "Crucify Jesus!" In our own year, things are hardly any different.

Most of us would prefer to consider ourselves as part of the crowd alongside the path into Jerusalem, but in all honesty we know that we are standing along the Way of the Cross often watching Jesus as He carries the Cross, sometimes mocking Him, and perhaps even taking pleasure as He falls three times. If our reaction is to say, "I would never do those things to Jesus," we might ask ourselves how many people we struggle to get along with in life, and how often we mock others' opinions, or take pleasure in their failures. *"Amen, I say to you, what you did not do for one of these least ones, you did not do for me"* [Matthew 25:45].

We shout a lot in life. We shout like the crowd along the Way of the Cross. But what are we doing to help Our Lord as He walks that path towards Calvary? We know that He must carry the Cross. If you walked up to Our Lord and asked Him to put the Cross down, He would not do so. This is how much He loves you.

Jesus knows that only by carrying the Cross—that Cross that by all rights is yours—can you ever have the chance to live in this world in peace, and forever in Heaven. Jesus knows that only by hanging upon the Cross to the point of expiration— giving up His last breath in the Holy Spirit—can you ever have the chance for the Holy Spirit to dwell within your own soul. Jesus knows that only by teaching you to carry a Cross for others will you ever make sense of this world, pass through it, and be led by Our Lord after death to the gates of Heaven.

So much of this world that we live in here below seems to consist of shouting. There are people crying for our attention, telling us what a great deal that they have for us. Everywhere we hear people shouting that they've found something that makes life easier: something that makes sense of this world. But in fact, Christ listens to none of the shouting around Him. He does not listen to those who cry "Hosanna!" He does not listen to those who cry "Crucify Him!" Before the crowds, he does not refute, he does not debate, he does not defend Himself. He simply continues his journey to the Cross in silence.

During this week, set aside time for silence. In silence, look into your conscience and prepare yourself for sacramental confession. In silence, read the Gospel accounts of Jesus' Passion, Death, and Resurrection. In silence, Christ invites us to join Him on His journey. He invites us to put back in its scabbard that two-edged sword.

Palm Sunday of the Passion of the Lord [B]
Isaiah 50:4-7 + Philippians 2:6-11 + Mark 14:1—15:47

"Eloi, Eloi, lema sabachthani?"

We might ask ourselves why Jesus prayed these words from Psalm 22 while nailed to the Cross. Did Jesus really feel abandoned by God the Father? How could God the Son ever not be loved by God the Father? Great spiritual masters have spilt much ink over this mystery, but any answer has to be based upon the very reason for the Crucifixion of the man-God: that is, God's sacrificial love for fallen man.

Jesus came into this world to be the Messiah of Israel: to be Israel's king, even given that Israel had fallen far as a people from their covenant with the LORD God. Jesus came into this world in solidarity with the fallen nation of Israel. We hear this connection between Jesus and Israel when we listen to the entire 22nd psalm. When we pray the entire 22nd psalm, we hear its spiritual current. The first words of the psalm—the words of today's Responsorial refrain, and the words the evangelist records Jesus crying from the Cross—are words of spiritual agony. *"My God, my God, why have you forsaken me?"*

Jesus cries these words as the King of Israel: as Israel's leader. Jesus cries these words as the experience of the people of Israel. The nation of Israel had felt abandoned by God. Of course, from our comfortable armchairs in the 21st century, we know that God had never abandoned Israel. Time and time again, just the opposite had shown itself to be the case: Israel had abandoned God. It's like the old saying, "If you feel that there's a distance between you and God, guess who has moved?" Nonetheless, as the leader of Israel, Jesus cries the cry of His people, but only to lead His people forward, out of their despair. This king wants to lead us in returning to God the Father, as the Prodigal Son returned to his father after coming to his senses [see Luke 15:11-32]. This king is even with us before we as sinners come to our senses: even when we blame God Himself for the distance between ourselves and Him.

The sinner King David, in composing this psalm, led his

people. As their king, David led Israel from the self-righteousness of the first verse—accusing God of abandoning His children—to the last verses that look beyond the individual's suffering, towards hope for an entire people. The psalm concludes by praying: *"And to him my soul shall live; / my descendants shall serve him. / Let the coming generation be told of the LORD / that they may proclaim to a people yet to be born / the justice he has shown"* [Psalm 22:31-32].

From the first verse to the last, you hear this spiritual current, running from self-righteous despair to righteous hope. So if Jesus spoke the first verse of this psalm on the Cross, He likely prayed the entire psalm on the Cross. Furthermore, what David could only sing about in words, Jesus accomplished through His self-sacrifice. Jesus leads us from self-righteousness to the righteousness of the Cross.

Many of us sinners find ourselves at times wallowing in self-pity. We cry over and over only the first verse of Psalm 22: *"My God, my God, why have you forsaken me?"* By contrast, from His Cross Jesus leads us in praying the entirety of Psalm 22, and accepting the offering of His life as the price for our sins. The sacrifice of the life is the price for our abandonment of God the Father.

But that's not the only context in which we ought to join our voices to Jesus' in praying Psalm 22. Not only do we need to pray the entirety of Psalm 22, from the first verse to the last. We need, in reaching the end of Psalm 22, to continue praying Sacred Scripture by taking up the next psalm.

Jesus spent many hours nailed to the Cross on Good Friday, until 3:00 p.m., the hour of Divine Mercy. During those many hours, do you imagine that He prayed only one psalm? If He prayed the entire 22nd psalm, then when he reached its end, don't you imagine that He continued praying from the Book of Psalms?

Is it a coincidence that Psalm 22 is followed by Psalm 23? As God directs one's spiritual life, there are no coincidences: only divine Providence. Each and every psalm has to be prayed within the setting of the entire Psalter of King David. All 150 psalms together make a single cry of fallen man to his covenantal LORD.

If you read and reflect on Psalm 22 during this Holy Week, continue your reading and reflection with the 23rd psalm. If Psalm 22 is the prayer of Palm Sunday and Good Friday, then Psalm 23 is the prayer of Easter Sunday morning, and indeed, the whole Easter Season. The depth of Jesus' suffering offers us hope, because through it, Jesus shepherds us so as to abide in Him, where there is nothing we shall want.

Palm Sunday of the Passion of the Lord [C]
Isaiah 50:4-7 + Philippians 2:6-11 + Luke 22:14—23:56

*Rather, he emptied himself
taking the form of a slave....*

No one likes being a slave. It's one thing to be an employee. In our own day and age an employee has rights, including the important right to walk off the job. It may have been a few years, but you've probably heard the country song whose title begins with the words "Take this job...." We like having the freedom to say those words, even if it's qualified by the real-life need to support ourselves and our families, whose well-being we don't want to jeopardize.

But an employee is very different from a slave. Real slavery offers no terms. Even indentured servitude is different than slavery because it offers in the here and now not freedom, but the hope of freedom. In the year 1670, a young man in England named John Horsington agreed to enter indentured servitude in exchange for passage to the New World. He served his time in what later became the state of Connecticut. I don't know how many years of freedom he enjoyed in the New World before his death, but he believed that those years of servitude were worth it, not only for his sake but also for the sake of his descendants.

But Jesus became a slave to sin for the sake of all mankind. Saying this is different, of course, than saying that Jesus sinned. Jesus, like His Mother, never committed sin, or inherited Original Sin. On the other hand, Saint Paul in his *Second Letter to the Corinthians* states that God the Father **"made [Jesus] to be sin who did not know sin"** [2 Corinthians 5:21]. It's in the light of this truth that today, on Palm Sunday, we need to look on Jesus as a slave to sin.

The difference between Jesus and us is that Jesus freely accepted the yoke of the Cross. On the other hand, sinful human beings—stretching from Adam and Eve to us—always accept slavery freely. Yet by sinning, we lose our very freedom. The devil whispered to Eve, "You shall be like gods!" Had he spoken the truth he would have told them "You shall be true slaves!"

Jesus, however, *"though he was in the form of God, / did not regard equality with God / something to be grasped. / Rather, he emptied himself, / taking the form of a slave...."*

In fact, the Church proclaims two Gospel passages on Palm Sunday. The first we hear before the Entrance Procession. It's a very optimistic, hopeful passage, proclaiming the triumphal entrance of the Messiah into Jerusalem. For century after century the Jews had longingly waited for the coming of the Messiah, and now Jesus seemed to make clear, by His entrance into the royal city, that He was the One.

But very soon after He arrived, things began to go downhill. The second Gospel proclamation on Palm Sunday stands in contrast to the first: not only in length, but also in tenor. The optimistic triumph of Jesus' procession into Jerusalem stands in contrast to the spite-filled mockery of Jesus' recession out of Jerusalem to the top of Calvary.

Jesus' descent into slavery is progressive. We can hear this progress—or rather, regress—in our own words. That is, when you see the Passion in the format shown in your hand missal or in the parish missalette—divided into spoken parts like the script of a play—the crowd's words reveal Jesus' descent. These words reveal the fickleness of the heart held slave to sin.

This "crowd"—whose words become our own—represents different persons. The first instance in St. Luke's account is at the table of the Last Supper, and the "crowd" consists of the apostles. Jesus asks them a question: *"When I sent you forth"* to do My work, *"were you [ever] in need of anything?"* The "crowd" replies, *"No, nothing".* The apostles said these two words with gratitude, surely, recognizing the generosity of Jesus.

From the apostles' gratitude it's all downhill, or rather uphill to Calvary. The next two times the "crowd" speaks, they speak about the sword. They want to defend Jesus, and in so doing prevent His Passion (prevent His vocation!). In response Jesus cries, *"Stop, no more of this!"* Soon after, though, the "crowd" speaks not in defense of Jesus, but accusing Peter of being one of Jesus' followers. When Peter flees, the "crowd" speaks in the name of the men who held Jesus in custody, beating and mocking Him with the words, *"Prophesy! Who is it that struck you?"*

The final four times that the "crowd" speaks, their mockery and contempt only grows. In seeing Jesus' patience in the midst of those who mock Him, we see the Lord Jesus submit as a slave to the sinners He came to free from slavery to sin. The "crowd" cries out for Pontius Pilate to release a guilty man, and to condemn the innocent Son of God. When Pilate hesitates, the "crowd"—representing all of sinful mankind—demands that their slave be killed: *"Crucify him! Crucify him!"*

The "crowd" speaks the last two times while Jesus is nailed to the cross that is yours. The "crowd" sneers at Jesus, *"He saved others, let him save himself if he is the chosen one, the Christ of God."* Offering Jesus wine, the "crowd" issues a command to the divine slave: *"If you are King of the Jews, save yourself."*

In those two words lie slavery to sin: *"Save yourself."* From Adam and Eve, to Jesus and Mary, to you and me, all of mankind has been tempted by those words: *"Save yourself."* Only Christ and His Blessed Mother never tried to put those words into practice. Every other member of the human race, from Adam and Eve to you and me, has tried to save himself and herself. "Tried"... and failed. Only God can save. The fact that Jesus was God, but did not save Himself on Calvary, reveals to us what life is supposed to be about. Life is not about saving our selves. It is not even about our selves. Trying to save our selves leads to death. In the words of St. Francis of Assisi, *"It is in dying that we are born to eternal life."*

Jesus, although He was and is God, did not save Himself, and in this He reveals to us what life is all about. Life... is about love. Love is about an other, not about my self.

MONDAY, TUESDAY & WEDNESDAY OF HOLY WEEK

Monday of Holy Week
Isaiah 42:1-7 + John 12:1-11

And the chief priests plotted to kill Lazarus too, because many of the Jews were turning away and believing in Jesus because of him.

Having entered into Jerusalem with Jesus, we recall the testimony about Jesus in Bethany, where Lazarus stands as a sign that arouses the wrath of the Jews. Lazarus probably laughed at the idea of being threatened by the Jews: he had already experienced death, and had been raised by Jesus. How could the Jews threaten him? They have no power over him.

We, too, must be willing to testify to the power of Our Lord over us. We must not fear those who threaten us in this world, for they have no power over us. They have power only over things that God has already called us to forsake, or to give to others.

At the beginning of this Holy Week, we see many people working against Jesus. In the end, His death was not an accident. But for every person who worked to nail Jesus to the Cross, there was a choice made, or many choices. We remember that on the Cross, Jesus prayed, *"Father, forgive them, they know not what they do"* [Luke 23:34]. Every one of us who is a sinner has the chance to accept this prayer. We have the chance to realize that even on the Cross, Jesus is our Good Shepherd, who wants to offer us His divine mercy and forgiveness.

Tuesday of Holy Week
Isaiah 49:1-6 + John 13:21-33,36-38

"Amen, amen, I say to you, one of you will betray me."

Today we hear the infamous promise of Saint Peter: *"Why can I not follow you now? I will lay down my life for you!"* Our Lord knows that Peter is too weak to keep this promise. *"The spirit is willing, but the flesh is weak"* [Matthew 26:41]. Yet Jesus does not disown Peter. Within this encounter of human frailty and divine compassion, we see the Lord's love for each of us reflected.

Despite the weakness of so many of His followers, Jesus does not abandon His intention to accomplish His Father's Will. Jesus is abandoned, but He will not abandon His Father's Will. Jesus still is willing to carry the Cross, for you in the same way as for His Blessed Mother, Saint Peter, and even for Judas Iscariot.

Perhaps the most striking action in today's Gospel is Judas Iscariot's betrayal of Our Lord. Jesus knows Judas better than Judas knows himself. Jesus knew that it would be by Judas' betrayal that He would be offered the Cross. But Jesus also knew that after his betrayal, Judas would refuse to turn back to the Lord for forgiveness, contrary to the desire of Jesus' compassionate Sacred Heart.

Certainly Judas' betrayal was more serious than Peter's. Nonetheless, Judas could have turned back to Jesus afterwards, and would have found in Jesus a merciful Redeemer. When Jesus said, *"Where I am going, you cannot follow me now, though you will follow later"*, these words could have applied to Judas as to any of the other apostles. It was Judas' own choice to leave the Lord and to hang himself which prevented him from following after Our Lord. Pray that in our sins, each of us will always turn to our loving Redeemer.

Wednesday of Holy Week
Isaiah 50:4-9 + Matthew 26:14-25

"...woe to that man by whom the Son of Man is betrayed."

For those of us who have been baptized, Christ is a gift that has been given to us. The meaning of our lives as Christians can be measured, then, by the way in which we use that gift. When we consider again the words of Our Lord— *"...woe to that man by whom the Son of Man is betrayed"*—we recognize that we too have betrayed the Son of Man. How often have we betrayed our baptismal promises: those promises we are preparing ourselves to renew at Easter?

But if we consider the word at the root of this phrase, we realize even more so how by our very nature we are bound to hand over Christ: not by betrayal, but by a "handing over" nonetheless. The Latin infinitive from which we derive the phrase "hand over"—*tradere*—is the same verb from which we derive the word "tradition", the source of transmitting the Catholic faith to all peoples through all ages.

How longingly Christ wants to be "handed over"! How lovingly Christ "hands over" to us on the altar of the Cross His Body and Blood, soul and divinity. Woe to us if—in receiving Christ—we do not hand him over. To whom ought we hand him over? Not to priests who will sacrifice Him to death, but to those who search for meaning in this world. Woe to us if we do not hand over to others the Truth that only in the Cross is meaning to be found.

HOLY THURSDAY —
MASS OF THE LORD'S SUPPER

Holy Thursday—Mass of the Lord's Supper
Exodus 12:1-8,11-14 + 1 Corinthians 11:23-26 + John 13:1-15

Before the feast of Passover, Jesus knew that his hour had come to pass from this world to the Father.

The Passover defines the Jewish people. Even in the present day, Jewish people throughout the world celebrate the Passover in commemoration of the miracles God worked for them some 3,500 years ago.

But the meaning of those original events may become jumbled in our minds. This jumbling might come from there being three passovers that occurred all those years ago. But for us as Christians, it's important to reflect on all three of these passovers, because all three of them foreshadow what Jesus chose to do for us during the Holy Week that ended with His death on Calvary.

The first of those three passovers is the focus of tonight's First Reading. Usually when we Christians—who don't understand the depth of Jewish culture—think about the Passover, we think about the Passover meal. The institution of this meal is described in tonight's First Reading. But to think of the Jewish Passover only as a meal is to miss the larger point.

If you've ever attended a Seder meal, which is a simpler form of the traditional Passover meal, you know that there are many items that are eaten and drunk. Each symbolizes some aspect of the Jewish escape from Egypt. But the element of the meal that is vital is the Passover lamb.

The *"lamb that was slain"* [Revelation 5:12] is the source of the blood of the first Passover. The Book of Exodus proclaims the words of the LORD to Moses and Aaron in Egypt: *"with the whole assembly of Israel present, [the lamb] shall be slaughtered during the evening twilight. They shall take some of its blood and apply it to the two doorposts and the lintel of every house...."*

This isn't animal sacrifice for the sake of giving God the first fruits of one's livestock. Nor is the lamb slaughtered as some sort of scapegoat for the people's sins. The purpose of slaying the lamb is entirely different: it's in order to protect those who mark their doors with the blood of this lamb. In this evening's First Reading we heard the LORD go on to explain this: *"It is the Passover of the Lord. For on this same night I will go through Egypt, striking down every firstborn of the land.... But the blood will mark the houses where you are. Seeing the blood, I will pass over you...."*

This is the first passing over: the Lord not striking dead those whose doors are marked by the Blood of the Lamb. The Lord passes over those who mark themselves with the blood of the lamb of the Passover meal. It doesn't take much reflection to see how this foreshadows Jesus' institution of the Eucharist on Holy Thursday: this night. Jesus is the Lamb who was slain for our salvation, and His Blood and Body, soul and divinity, which the Lord invites His faithful to receive in the Eucharist, brings us salvation from the eternal death caused by sin.

The second passing over in Egypt all those thousands of years ago was the passing over of the Red Sea. This second passover was some time later than the Passover meal, but it's a consequence of the first, and makes possible the third passover. In the Book of Exodus, the account of passing over the Red Sea comes just two chapters after the chapter this evening's First Reading is taken from. The account of God's people passing over the Red Sea will be proclaimed just two nights from now at the Easter Vigil.

The third passing over all those thousands of years ago was the passing over from Egypt—through the wilderness—to the land flowing with milk and honey: the passing over from slavery to freedom. This third passing over required forty years of wandering, and the Bible takes three and a half books of the

Bible to recount that third passover. If the first of those original passovers foreshadows the Sacrament of the Eucharist, and the second of them foreshadows the Sacrament of Baptism, then this third passover foreshadows the whole of our Christian life in this valley of tears, which for some of us is much longer than forty years, but full of even more wandering than the Lord's People in the wilderness.

With all the modern discoveries of historians, we still are not sure where exactly the Pharaoh who enslaved the Israelites lived all those thousands of years ago. Nor can we be certain about the location where the Lord's People, forty years after their escape from Egypt, crossed over the Jordan River into the Promised Land. Still, if we estimate this distance by measuring from the city of Cairo in Egypt to the city of Jerusalem, we end up with a distance of about 310 miles. That's the approximate distance from Enid, Oklahoma to Kansas City, Missouri.

So we have to ask: how could it possibly have taken the Hebrews forty years to travel 310 miles? As we consider an answer, we need to remember that the entirety of the Old Testament, and most particulars within it, foreshadow Christ and the Christian life. In the biblical books that narrate the third passover from Egypt, through the wilderness to the Promised Land, God makes clear that it's in punishment for their infidelity and lack of trust in Him that He prevents them from making this Passover in a straight line. He causes them to meander, to retrace their steps countless times. He demands that they learn patience, humility and trust in His providential guidance. Obviously, in the Lord's punishment, the one who is punished grows closer to God if he accepts his punishment with faith and in humility.

The parallels between this forty-year passover and the Christian spiritual life are clear. The land of Egypt symbolizes the fallen world and the Christian's slavery to sin. The Promised Land is Heaven. In between is the forty-year trek that symbolizes the ups and downs of the earthly spiritual life: two steps forward followed by one step back, and sometimes even one step forward and two steps back.

In the midst of the original passover from Egypt to the

Promised Land, the Hebrews celebrated the annual Passover meal forty times. They were also, however, gifted by the Lord with manna from Heaven.

At His Last Supper, Jesus instituted the Sacrament of the Eucharist and the Sacrament of the Priesthood. Throughout the almost two thousand years of the Church, as the Church Militant has trekked through history like the Hebrews through the wilderness, the Most Blessed Sacrament of the Eucharist is the heavenly manna that has fortified His people for the struggle of the earthly journey.

The Eucharist defines God's Church. We give thanks this evening for this gift. We give thanks that every single day of the year except Good Friday, the Holy Sacrifice of the Mass is celebrated, and each of us has the opportunity to receive worthily the Body and Blood, soul and divinity of Jesus Christ. What Jesus offered on the Cross, you have the opportunity to share in, 364 days a year. It's pride to think that we can be faithful followers of Jesus without His help. It's humility that allows the Lord to wash us clean, and to strengthen us with His own Self for the on-going journey that we have before us.

GOOD FRIDAY

Good Friday
Isaiah 52:13—53:12 + Hebrews 4:14-16;5:7-9 + John 18:1—19:42

*We had all gone astray like sheep, / each following his own way; /
but the LORD laid upon him / the guilt of us all.*

When Jesus had finished celebrating the First Mass—when
He had handed over the banquet of His Last Supper to His
twelve apostles, for them to celebrate from then on—Jesus had
only one thing more to give to His followers. From the Upper
Room, Jesus set out to give this final gift.

The journey from that Upper Room to the top of Calvary
was the longest journey that Jesus ever made. It wasn't
physically the longest: physically, it would not have taken long
to walk from the Upper Room to the top of Calvary. But it was
the longest journey that Jesus ever made because in that journey,
He had to give up everything that's humanly important.

Sometimes, what seems like a small thing can be very
difficult to give up. Think of a time when you've hurt someone
because of what you said or did. You know that you need to say
those simple words: "I'm sorry." All you have to do is open
your mouth and pronounce them. It's not that you don't know
how to do that.

It's not that there's a great difficulty in finding the person
you need to say those words to: usually, the persons we hurt the
most are those who are closest to us. The person you need to
say those words to may be in the very next room from where
you're sitting at home in the evening. Yet how difficult it is to
get up out of your chair, walk ten steps, and speak those words.

That journey of yours, which is a journey not just made by your feet, but also made with your heart and mind, can be extremely long. It can take some people decades to make that journey.

Jesus, of course, didn't make His journey to Calvary because He needed to say, "I'm sorry". Jesus had nothing to be sorry for. Even the criminal who would hang on the cross to Jesus' right could see that.

Jesus didn't make the journey to Calvary because of His sins, but because of our sins. Jesus made the journey to Calvary in order to become sin [see 2 Corinthians 5:21]. Jesus gave up all the rights and privileges of being God in order to become sin in that sense that St. Paul writes about. Jesus takes into Himself every human sin, committed by every human being, in every place, at every moment of human life: past, present and future.

Jesus' journey from the Upper Room to Calvary, then, was not so much a physical journey, as it was a moral and spiritual journey, over the course of which He went from being God's beloved and innocent Son to becoming sin. In His humanity, would Jesus have wanted to make this journey? What would have moved Jesus?

Jesus goes straight from the Upper Room to the Garden of Gethsemane, His first resting place on this journey. It's there that He's betrayed. But which do you think, humanly speaking, hurt Jesus more: His betrayal by Judas Iscariot, whose betrayal was foretold by Scripture, or His betrayal by the ten apostles who fled from Jesus when He was arrested? Whose betrayal would have pained Jesus more: that of Judas, or that of Peter, James, Thomas, Philip, and all of the others?

In the midst of eleven of His twelve apostles betraying Him, what would Jesus have felt? And how would Jesus' journey have changed at that moment? Not the moment of His arrest, but the moment in which those eleven apostles flew in all different directions? At that moment, Jesus saw that His closest companions would not walk His journey with Him. Do you think, humanly speaking, that Jesus would have been tempted not to continue His journey? What would have moved Jesus to press on?

During the hours of His arrest, as humiliation, torment, and physical torture were added to abandonment, what would have moved Jesus from within? Throughout the experiences of His Passion, Jesus could have called upon legions of angels to fly down from Heaven, smite His persecutors, and raise Him to Heaven. Why did He not do so? Why did He choose instead to look into the eyes of the Roman soldiers, and say in His Heart, "I am making this journey for you, also. I want to open the gates of Heaven, so that you can enter through them into eternal life"?

Jesus didn't make His journey just for those who stood by His side. Jesus didn't make this journey just for His Blessed Mother, for Lazarus, Martha and Mary, for his foster-father Joseph, His cousin John the Baptizer, and His grandparents Joachim and Anne.

Jesus made this journey for the soldier who pushed the crown of thorns down into his head. Jesus made this journey for those who lashed His back, and tore off His flesh. Jesus made this journey for the soldiers who drove spikes through His hands and His feet. For each one of them, Jesus said with His lips, *"Father, forgive them, they know not what they do"* [Luke 23:34]. Jesus said from His Heart, "Father, I give up everything I have, in order to take their sins into my very being. I want to become their sins, so that their sins will die, instead of them."

When Jesus became sin and died on the Cross, sin died. The power of sin lost its power. At the moment that Jesus, weighted down with the sins of all mankind, breathed His last, His soul left His Body. As the Apostles' Creed states: "He descended into Hell". This is not the place reserved for the fallen angels and damned human beings, but that spiritual abode where the just had to wait for the Messiah to lead them to Heaven.

Within this abode of the dead, which is sometimes called "Hades", Jesus found the "saints" of the Old Testament, as well as His foster-father Joseph, John the Baptist, and others. None of them could enter Heaven, no matter how good his life on earth might have been, because the gates of Heaven had been locked shut from the day of Adam and Eve's Original Sin, and could only be opened by God's only-begotten Son.

In their midst, Jesus said to the just what He said to His tormenters: "I have made this journey for you." He says this to every human being: past, present and future. Those who place their faith in Jesus rise with Him, just as Jesus, raised up by God the Father's love, rose to Heaven, where He opened the gates of Heaven for all of the just who chose to place their faith in the God-man Jesus Christ.

Jesus has died. He became sin, and died on the Cross, so that your sins would be put to death: that is, so that your sins would no longer have power over your life. But you have to accept Jesus with faith in your heart. Like the just souls in Hell, you have to believe Jesus when He says, "I have made this journey for you."

HOLY SATURDAY — MORNING

Holy Saturday
Hebrews 4:1-13

It is we who have believed who enter into that rest, just as God said....

No Mass may be celebrated today until darkness has fallen. Then the Vigil of the Lord's Resurrection may begin. Throughout most of this day, the Church meditates upon the death that God suffered for us, and upon His descent into the underworld. The Church celebrates the Sacred Liturgy during the early part of today through the Liturgy of the Hours. Consider the New Testament passage that the Church proclaims today in the Office of Readings, from Chapter 4 of the *Letter to the Hebrews.*

If there's one word that sums up this passage, it would be *"rest".* The one phrase that sums it up: *"It is we who have believed who enter into that rest".* But what exactly is this rest that we enter through belief?

There are two Old Testament contexts for this passage from *Hebrews.* The first is the creation account from *Genesis*, at the end of which we hear that *"God blessed the seventh day and made it holy, because on it he rested from all the work he had done in creation"* [Genesis 2:3]. This passage is mentioned by the author of *Hebrews* only briefly, though. He moves beyond it to the Exodus.

The second Old Testament context is Psalm 95, in which the Psalmist sings of the Exodus retrospectively. He looks back at the wilderness of the Exodus and contrasts it with the land of milk and honey which Joshua led Israel into so that there they might find rest. The author of *Hebrews* points out, though, that this rest is only a foreshadowing of the rest of which he speaks.

Consider, then, the liturgical context for this *"rest"* that Christians have entered into by believing. As today is Holy Saturday, the death of Jesus is plainly the immediate liturgical context. As His Body rests in its tomb, we keep vigil. But this rest of Jesus is also a foreshadowing.

So what type of rest do all these contexts point towards?

We would have good reason to answer, "The rest of the Risen Christ", but we would have to offer this answer with a reservation. Although in meditating on the death of the God-man we await the victory of His Resurrection, the Risen Lord remains on earth for only forty days. He ascends to Heaven so that from there He and the Father might send the Gift of the Holy Spirit.

The Power of the Holy Spirit impels us to carry out the work of the Church: the work of the new creation. Doing so we draw others into the life of the "good things" of the Church: not milk and honey, but water, blood and the spirit. All of this on earth prepares us for our final rest, which the Father calls us into through the door of death: a life of rest in the bosom of Father, Son and Holy Spirit.

HOLY SATURDAY — THE EASTER VIGIL

The Easter Vigil in the Holy Night of Easter
Genesis 1:1—2:2 + Genesis 22:1-18 + Exodus 14:15—15:1 +
Isaiah 54:5-14 + Isaiah 55:1-11 + Baruch 3:9-15, 32-4:4 +
Ezekiel 36:16-17a, 18-28 + Romans 6:3-11 + [Year A] Matt 28:1-10
+ [Year B] Mark 16:1-7 + [Year C] Luke 24:1-12

For if we have grown into union with him through a death like his, we
shall also be united with him in the resurrection.

When we stand and sum up, out loud, what it is we believe as
Christians, one of the first things we say about God is that He is
"creator": as in, "I believe in God, the Father almighty, Creator
of Heaven and earth".

We hear of God as Creator in the first words of Sacred
Scripture. The First Reading at the Easter Vigil tells us how
God creates: **"In the beginning, when God created the heavens and**
the earth, the earth was a formless wasteland...." In other words,
God is able to take nothing, and make something out of it.

This is not the heart of our Christian faith, but it is the
beginning: God can take nothing, and make something out of it.

You and I cannot do that. Human beings cannot create
something out of nothing. We can create. One of the most
powerful ways that we grow in our Christian Faith is through
human works of creation: human art. Christian art can be very
simple. When we pray the Stations of the Cross, for example,
and hold that little booklet in our hands, the picture on the left-
hand side of the page helps us to see, in the simple beauty of its
art, what the words on the right-hand side help us to say out
loud.

Art is everywhere in our Catholic Faith. Statues, paintings and pictures all help us to grow in the Faith. We know, too, that there are masterpieces in museums and churches, in states and countries far from where we live our every-day lives, that stun the imagination. In the whole of our lives, we may only have one chance to see, for example, Michelangelo's Pietà in St. Peter's Basilica in Rome. But if we do see it, even once, it has a great impact on our life: years later, we will still talk about it to others, and try to express how beautiful and captivating it is. We may not express this beauty very well, but we are never the same after we see it, all because Michelangelo chose to create this particular human work of art.

The difference, of course, between the way that God creates and the way that humans create is an infinite difference. God creates out of nothing. Humans have to have a "something" in front of them in order to produce a work of art. The sculptor needs a block of marble, as well as a chisel, as well as a lot of free time to work. The painter needs brushes, palettes, paints, a canvas, as well as a lot of time. But God creates out of nothing, in less than a moment, in less than a snap of the fingers.

There's another difference between God as The Creator and the different ways that we humans approach creation. This difference is in the approaches we take to "broken creation". What do we humans do when something breaks? In our modern Western culture, especially in the United States, our knee-jerk reaction to something breaking is to throw it away and to buy a new one. Whether it's a lamp, a printer, or a coffee maker, when something breaks, it no longer seems to have value. There's no reason to keep it around.

If we do try to fix something, there's no guarantee that we'll have much success. Growing up with two sisters and a brother, I can only remember once—apart from making too much noise in the car—that all four of us got in trouble for the same thing. The trouble was because of our mother's favorite lamp: an Oriental lamp that, one day, got right in the way of someone's beeline during a game of indoor Tag. I don't know which was greater: our fear of our mother's reaction, or our self-delusion that we could put the five hundred pieces back together. Maybe because of fear, though, we tried as hard as we could to fit all the pieces back into a whole.

Whether it's in regard to a lamp, car, clock or computer, our ability to fix—our ability to "re-create"—something that is broken is limited. That ability depends upon our knowledge, technical savvy and experience.

But there are some things that we simply cannot fix: not through our own human powers. These are the things that become broken because of sin and death in this world. No matter how much we wish and no matter how much we try, we cannot fix and cannot put back together what has been torn apart by sin and death. We try to persuade ourselves otherwise. But we fail.

By ourselves, we fail. With God, we succeed. This is the Good News of Jesus' Resurrection. *"We were indeed buried with [Jesus] through baptism into death, so that, just as Christ was raised from the dead by the glory of the Father, we too might live in newness of life."*

God creates differently than we create, and God re-creates in a different way, too. God can do what we cannot. God can forgive sins: bringing about grace in the soul of someone who has rejected Him. God can raise up those who have died, as the Son of God proclaims to us today. God can bring life out of death.

This is not just a promise about the future, based on hope. This is not only admiring what God the Father did for Jesus 2000 years ago: something to believe with faith. Through the Eucharist, the Risen Jesus—His glorified Body and Body, soul and divinity—enter into the person who receives Him. The grace of this Sacrament, if we accept it and allow it to change us, is what gives us the chance to let God re-create our lives.

This grace is what changes not tomorrow—not yesterday— but today. This grace is what allows us to love, in our daily life, those whom we find it difficult to love, whether that is someone we keep at a distance, someone very close to us, or even our own self. This grace is what allows us to love as God has loved us, and to live in that love even after our death in this world, to enjoy the presence of God all His saints for eternity.

EASTER SUNDAY
OF THE RESURRECTION OF THE LORD

Easter Sunday of the Resurrection of the Lord
Acts 10:34,37-43 + Colossians 3:1-4 + John 20:1-9

So Peter and the other disciple went out and came to the tomb.

As Christians, we believe that life always demands sacrifice. Whereas the world around us believes that life is followed by death, we Christians believe that it's the other way around. Death is followed by life, and this truth is possible because of Jesus' sacrifice on the Cross.

In the deepest sense, that's what this most holy season of Easter is about: that the Passion and Death of Jesus bear fruit in His Resurrection. This is why the Church during this Easter Season cries, "Alleluia!" "Alleluia!" means, "Praise be to the Lord!"

We give praise to this Lord who raised Jesus from the dead because we see in Him the fruit of self-sacrifice. The fruits of Jesus' self-sacrifice are infinite, because He is God. But we also take this truth and want to live it out in our own lives. Although the fruits of your self-sacrifice or mine will never be infinite as are Jesus', we imitate Him nonetheless. Furthermore, we're only able to do so through the power of Jesus' self-sacrifice.

All of this can be hard to wrap our minds around. That's one reason why Easter is not just the single day of Easter Sunday, but a season of seven weeks plus one more day. The Church celebrates Easter for fifty days so as to ponder thoroughly the mysteries of this holiest season of the Church year. There are three mysteries of our Faith that the Church focuses upon especially during Easter. They are the first three Glorious Mysteries of the Rosary. But for now, just consider the first and third.

The first mystery is the focus of today: Easter Sunday, the first of the fifty days of Easter. This mystery is presented by today's Gospel passage. This passage presents the young apostle John as a model of how to ponder.

St. John, who was apostle and evangelist, accomplished all he did because he was the Beloved Disciple. As an apostle and an evangelist he served the Church as a zealous Martha, but only because first he was a faithful Mary. The Beloved Disciple at the Last Supper took the stance that Mary did at the meal in her home: sitting and listening at the feet of the Word made Flesh.

In many churches, you see above the high altar the youngest of the apostles—St. John—at one side of the Cross, and our Blessed Mother on the other. This is the scene of the Crucifixion that the Church celebrated just days ago.

But on the third day, this same John ran with Peter to the tomb. Along with Saint Peter and the Beloved Disciple, Saint John, we also see *"the burial cloths there."* John *"saw and believed."* With no sign of Jesus, and without a word from Jesus, John saw and believed simply because the tomb is empty. It is ironic that on the greatest feast of the Christian year, Christ doesn't even appear in this Gospel passage, nor speak a word. We see only His empty tomb, and we only hear silence.

Throughout this great season of Easter, we will be hearing many passages from the Gospel according to John. This is the apostle who alone among the Twelve stood at the foot of the Cross, and who on Easter morning saw an empty tomb and believed.

Saint John was the only one of the apostles who was not martyred. He lived until the close of the first Christian century, and it was in his last years, as an old man, that John wrote his three New Testament letters, his Gospel account, and the *Book of Revelation*. The Good News that John preached came from his remembering these two scenes, which no other apostle saw as he did. Saint John saw his Savior hanging on the Cross, and he saw the empty tomb and believed. He believed in the sacrifice of the Word made Flesh.

John's love was based upon a faith that did not need to Jesus Risen in the flesh. This great love is the love that John is teaching us to pray for during this Easter season.

John teaches us to pray during these fifty days of Easter for a great gift. God has a gift ready for us: the Gift of the Holy Spirit. That is why we hear every day of the Easter Season from the *Acts of the Apostles*, the book that describes the Church at work through the Power of the Holy Spirit. The descent of the Holy Spirit at Pentecost is the culminating mystery of Easter. We don't simply celebrate it on the last day of Easter as an afterthought: it is the mystery that Jesus leads us towards through His Resurrection.

We in our own day, through the Holy Spirit, become the members of His Body, the Church. Through this Holy Spirit, we continue Jesus' Mission of telling others—through our own sacrifices—that God has Good News for every human person: that God is more powerful than sin, despair, and death, and that He can strengthen us in this life to serve others, so as to be happy with Him in the next.

This is what we promise through the vows of our baptism. As in Holy Matrimony, these vows run two ways. The Church is the bride, and Jesus is the groom. Through the vows that He spoke on the Cross, Jesus makes a promise to us: that He will always offer His life to us through the Power of the Spirit.

SOLEMNITIES CELEBRATED DURING THE SEASON OF LENT

St. Joseph, Spouse of the Blessed Virgin Mary
II Samuel 7:4-5,12-14,16 + Romans 4:13,16-18,22 + Matthew 1:16,18-21,24 [or Luke 2:41-51]

The Solemnity of St. Joseph, Spouse of the Blessed Virgin Mary is traditionally observed on March 19. However, if that date falls on one of the first five Sundays of Lent, the solemnity is transferred to the following day. St. Joseph's feast is transferred to the day before Palm Sunday if March 19 falls during Holy Week.

When Joseph awoke, he did as the angel of the Lord had commanded him....

Saint Joseph has two chief feast days during the Church year. On May first we celebrate the feast of Saint Joseph the Worker. The Church on that day reflects especially upon how St. Joseph shows the great dignity in such an ordinary thing as work. This feast is relatively minor. In fact, that celebration is technically called an "optional memorial" that does not have to be observed at the day's Mass.

On March 19th, however, the Church celebrates Saint Joseph as the husband of Mary. This feast has the rank of "solemnity", which is the highest rank a feast can have within the Church's calendar. The Church today celebrates the fidelity that's reflected in the life of this man Joseph. The readings of today's feast draw our minds to the enduring nature of the covenant between the Lord and His People.

On a day-to-day basis, most of us have difficulty even remembering the small things that we promise to do for others. If I have to be reminded only once of something I've promised to do, I'm having a very good day. Of course, all of these small promises that we make are concrete examples of the promises by which we have consecrated our very lives to the Lord: first in baptism, and then in more specific vows or promises for those who are married, are consecrated religious, or are in Holy Orders. This promise of oneself—this faithful handing over of one's own earthly life to another—is the greatest covenant we can establish as individuals. It is by this that we become more than individuals. As such individuals, we bow in homage before the Lord who wishes to make this covenant with every human person who lives.

Because it's as the spouse of the Blessed Virgin Mary that we honor Saint Joseph today, today is in a sense a Marian feast. It is the spousal nature of Joseph's life that mirrors in his earthly life the enduring fidelity of the Lord God Himself. From his place in Heaven, St. Joseph is the patron of the universal Church, that instrument through which the Lord wishes to make a covenant with each member of the human race, making each person a member of His divine Son's Body. It is the Church that proclaims to the world yet converted the faithfulness of the Lord. It is the Church that proclaims to the world yet converted the faithfulness of the Lord, and it is the Church that is given by the Lord the promise that He will strengthen us in all the trials and even failures of our vocations within the Church.

The life of Saint Joseph is one of silent fidelity to the Lord. We have in Scripture no words of St. Joseph recorded. Even the words that are spoken by others to St. Joseph are words that measure by measure call for ever-growing trust in the Lord's plan. Step-by-step: that's the only way to reach Heaven. As we continue to walk the path to Calvary during Lent, let us pray that Saint Joseph's spousal trust and fidelity will be our own.

The Annunciation of the Lord
Isaiah 7:10-14;8:10 + Hebrews 10:4-10 + Luke 1:26-38

The Annunciation is traditionally observed on March 25. If that date falls on one of the first five Sundays of Lent, the solemnity is transferred to the following day. However, if March 25 falls during Holy Week or the Octave of Easter, the Annunciation is transferred to Monday of the Second Week of Easter.

"Behold, I am the handmaid of the Lord."

Nine months before the Church celebrates the Nativity of the Lord, she celebrates His conception within the womb of the Blessed Virgin Mary. We should not be distracted by the fact that this solemnity of the Annunciation falls each year during Lent or Easter. Rather, we ought to reflect on the relationship between today's feast and the holy seasons of Lent and Easter.

How is the Lord Jesus' conception related to His Death and Resurrection? Are they no more than ends of a spectrum? In fact, both are about new life. They draw our attention to, and celebrate, the unity of the person of Jesus Christ. They celebrate the unity of His humanity and divinity in His divine Person.

On a merely natural level, the reason for celebrating the Annunciation of our Lord on this day of March 25th is simple: March 25th is nine months before December 25th, and so nine months before celebrating the birth of the Word made Flesh, we celebrate the annunciation of that Word to Mary, and the acceptance of that Word into her heart and soul and womb.

On a deeper level, however, we see something even more mysterious occurring in the holy exchange between Saint Gabriel and the Blessed Virgin Mary. We realize that there is a reason much deeper than mere chronology for celebrating the Annunciation during the midst of Lent.

In the person of Jesus Christ, God and man are united. This is the good news that Saint Gabriel came to announce to Mary: that she would bear in her womb the one through whom all human beings could find not only meaning in their earthly lives, but eternal life in Heaven. The profundity of this news overwhelmed Mary and made her fearful. What would this mean for her life?

Throughout the world and throughout history, human beings have sought to find meaning in their lives in many ways. Similarly, human beings have always searched for love in their lives. We know that there are many different things which people in the world call love, but Jesus Christ and the Church He established upon this earth clearly teach us that there is only one real type of love: that love which over many years would lead Mary to Calvary. Only this real love is strong enough to destroy death, and only this real love is strong enough to bind together a man and a woman for life.

One of the titles that the Church has given to Our Lady is "Spouse of the Holy Spirit". This metaphor can help us reflect upon the event of the Annunciation as a type of marriage. If Mary had understood everything happening to her, she—like a young bride on the night before her wedding—might have feared the annunciation of Saint Gabriel even more than she did.

Both the Annunciation and its consummation on Calvary are sacred events which call us to consider how God expects us to accept the Holy Spirit in humble submission to the will of God. Mary is the greatest disciple of Our Lord. Beyond her questioning, she says *"Fiat"*: **"May it be done to me according to your word."** She accepts the fullness of the Holy Spirit and bears the Body of Christ, and so is the model for us who strive faithfully to say to God, "Into your hands, O Lord, I commend my spirit."

Those who have received the gifts of the Holy Spirit in Baptism and have had them strengthened in Confirmation turn to Mary, asking her intercession during their journey towards Calvary, and asking for perseverance to pray beneath the Cross. Those who have received the Sacrament of Holy Matrimony ask Mary's intercession, that they may always be faithful spouses, striving for what God wants for their spouses. May our devout and worthy reception of the Body and Blood of Christ help us to be transformed in mind and heart.

IN HONOR OF THE FIFTIETH
ANNIVERSARY OF *HUMANAE VITAE*

The Sixteenth Sunday in Ordinary Time [B]
Jeremiah 23:1-6 + Ephesians 2:13-18 + Mark 6:30-34
July 22, 2018

Woe to the shepherds who mislead and scatter the flock of my pasture,
says the LORD.

Discord is part and parcel of life in this fallen world. The great English author G. K. Chesterton once said that Original Sin is the simplest of all Christian dogmas to prove: all you have to do is pick up the newspaper, or click on a news app. In contrast to the discord of the fallen world, we fallen and redeemed Christians are called into unity and to foster unity.

Jesus told us simply to love God, and to love our neighbor. We can consider these two great commands in terms of being called into unity, and being called to foster unity. To love God is to be united with God, and to love one's neighbor ultimately means that all the members of the human race would foster unity with each other, forming a single family of God's children.

Yet if today this seems beyond us, we ought to recall that the first generations of Christians struggled with these two commands of love. Today's Second Reading offers a case in point. St. Paul is preaching against the division between Jews and Gentiles in the city of Ephesus. Throughout his entire letter to the Ephesians, St. Paul preaches about unity, and about where this unity must come from. Paul points to Christ, because Christ *"is our peace, he who made both one and broke down the dividing wall of enmity, through his flesh… [so] that he might create in himself one new person in place of the two, thus establishing peace"*.

Lasting peace can only come from unity through Christ. This is true in every aspect of life, but perhaps nowhere more so than in the vocation of Holy Matrimony. Christ Himself instructs His disciples—when He's questioned about what's wrong with divorce—that *"from the beginning the Creator 'made them male and female' and… 'For this reason a man shall leave his father and mother and be joined to his wife, and the two shall become one flesh'"* [Matthew 19:4-5, quoting Genesis 1:27;2:24].

This call to unity can be broken not only by divorce, though. Much more common in our Western culture is a sin that is praised by some—strangely enough—as an act of responsibility and even prudence: that is, the sin of artificial contraception.

+ + +

Fifty years ago this Wednesday, a watershed event took place amidst a generational deluge of change. On July 25, 1968, Blessed Pope Paul VI promulgated the encyclical letter *Humanae Vitae*. The Pope's teaching was not new. In fact, his teaching was not his, in the sense that he was not its author. *Humanae Vitae*'s teaching is consistent with the prior 1900 years of Church teaching upon the encyclical's chief topics. In other words, the teaching of this encyclical is the teaching of Jesus Christ. In giving this teaching to His Bride, the Church, Jesus has given of Himself, to reveal to His bride how to share in His own self-sacrificial love.

Humanae Vitae focuses upon three chief topics: human nature, the nature of marriage, and specifically the morality of artificial means of contraception. Those three are the chief lenses through which one must read, ponder, and pray over the encyclical. In considering the encyclical's teaching about any one of these three, the other two have to be kept in mind. It's much easier to dismiss the prophetic teaching of *Humanae Vitae* if you claim that it's "only" about the morality of artificial contraception.

Why has *Humanae Vitae* seemed so controversial since Blessed Paul VI promulgated it? A first reason is that so many

Christian denominations had since 1930 changed their teachings to suggest that using artificial contraception could sometimes be morally acceptable. By the 1960's, then, the Catholic Church seemed behind the times. In the first months of 1968 there was a widespread expectation that with *Humanae Vitae*, the Catholic Church would finally get "with it".

Blessed Paul VI determined, however, that it's better for the Church to be with Christ than to be "with it", which in any given generation is nothing but a shifting tide of public opinion. To be with Christ is to share in His self-sacrificial love.

The Church's teachings in this field, enriched so greatly over the past decades by St. John Paul the Great, show that planning a family according to natural means bestows not only moral and spiritual benefits upon wife, husband, and their shared married life. Planning a family according to natural means also has medical benefits, while artificial means of contraception are showing, more and more over time, how much physical harm can come from choosing what is artificial.

More and more people realize that they deserve better. Many are realizing that that "something better" comes from God Himself, in the order of nature by which He designed man and woman. As secular culture continues to fragment, and as more broken homes lead to more broken lives and to more crime, poverty, drug abuse and homelessness, the leaders of the Church are calling us back to the basics. The Church needs to go back to the heart of things to recover a way of life that has been mocked and abused in our secular culture for too long: a life of modesty, purity, and chastity.

Many in our culture are only waking up now to the hard truth about the consequences of believing that it's beneficial for a couple to separate the act of marital love from the openness of that act to conception. Many in our culture are only realizing now what happens when, for decades, a culture claims that this act has no intrinsic connection to child-bearing. Many are only realizing now that a culture that claims that marriage doesn't have to be open to the bearing of children is a culture that believes itself free to redefine marriage.

+ + +

Nonetheless, the secular culture is never going to be convinced of the truth of what the Church teaches unless the Church's members embrace and live out the Church's beliefs about Marriage and family life. The leaders of our Church see that. Of course, these same leaders also see the warnings in today's First Reading from the prophetic *Book of Jeremiah*. The prophet Jeremiah's warning is to worldly *"shepherds who mislead and scatter the flock of"* the LORD's pasture. The prophet cries out in the name of the LORD, saying to those unfaithful shepherds: *"You have scattered my sheep and driven them away. ... but I will take care to punish your evil deeds. I myself will gather the remnant of my flock from all the lands... and bring them back to their meadow; there they shall increase and multiply."* We in the modern Western world need to admit that this meadow is not the materialism promoted in the mass media. This meadow is the *"verdant pastures"* and *"restful waters"* of the spiritual and moral teachings of Jesus Christ, handed down to us by Jesus' Bride, the Church.

Yet the prophet Jeremiah also promises that the LORD's flock will be given faithful shepherds. The prophet cries out in the name of the LORD, declaring: *"I will appoint shepherds for them who will shepherd them so that they need no longer fear and tremble; and none shall be missing"*. Sadly, too many children are missing in our world today because we've accepted the secular culture's claim that divorcing the act of physical union from an openness to conception bears no consequences. But the consequences continue to mount all around us.

The remedy for a culture that canonizes barrenness, self-promotion, and immediate satisfaction of one's every desire is the Way of our Good Shepherd, Jesus Christ. As a Christian, you must never kid yourself into thinking that this Way is easy, broad and comfortable. After all, your life is not about you: as the Psalmist sings in the 23rd Psalm, *"He guides me in right paths for his name's sake."* About those *"right paths"* we need to remember what Jesus explained to us: *"How narrow the gate and constricted the road that leads to life. And those who find it are few"* [Matthew 7:14]. Nonetheless, take comfort in the truth that if you follow the Good Shepherd on this narrow Way, you *"shall dwell in the house of the LORD / for years to come."*

Litany to the Bishop Martyrs
for the Bishops of the Church Militant

This Litany is for private use only.
It is not approved for use within the Sacred Liturgy.

Lord, have mercy.   *Lord, have mercy.*
Christ, have mercy.   *Christ, have mercy.*
Lord, have mercy.   *Lord, have mercy.*
Christ, hear us.   *Christ, graciously hear us.*

God the Father of heaven,   *have mercy on us.*
God the Son, Redeemer of the world,   *have mercy on us.*
God the Holy Spirit,   *have mercy on us.*
Holy Trinity, one God,   *have mercy on us.*

Our Lady, Queen of Martyrs,   *pray for them.*
Our Lady, Queen of Popes,   *pray for them.*
Our Lady, Queen of Bishops,   *pray for them.*
Pope Saint Fabian,   *pray for them.*
Pope Saint Martin I,   *pray for them.*
Pope Saint John I,   *pray for them.*
Pope Saint Sixtus II,   *pray for them.*
Pope Saint Pontian,   *pray for them.*
Pope Saint Cornelius,   *pray for them.*
Pope Saint Callistus I,   *pray for them.*
Pope Saint Clement I,   *pray for them.*
Saint Blaise,   *pray for them.*
Saint Polycarp,   *pray for them.*
Saint Stanislaus,   *pray for them.*
Saint Adalbert,   *pray for them.*
Saint Boniface,   *pray for them.*
Saint John Fisher,   *pray for them.*
Saint Irenaeus,   *pray for them.*

Saint Apollinaris,   *pray for them.*
Saint Cyprian,   *pray for them.*
Saint Januarius,   *pray for them.*
Saint Ignatius of Antioch,   *pray for them.*
Saint Josaphat,   *pray for them.*
Saint Thomas Becket,   *pray for them.*

Lamb of God, Who takes away the sins of the world,
                              spare us, O Lord.
Lamb of God, Who takes away the sins of the world,
                              graciously hear us, O Lord.
Lamb of God, Who takes away the sins of the world,
                              have mercy on us.

Pray for us, all you Shepherds who have laid down your lives
for the sheep,

                              that we may be made worthy of
                              the promises of Christ.

Let us pray.
O God our Providential Father, look upon the Bishops of your
Church on earth in union with the Supreme Pontiff, and
increase in them the virtue of fortitude. Through the
intercession of those Holy Shepherds who have already spilled
their blood in witness of the Gospel, grant, if your shepherds be
struck or struck down, that the sheep may not scatter, but that
they may be one, in faith and in the Truth, Who is Jesus Christ
our Lord, Who lives and reigns with You, in the unity of the
Holy Spirit, one God forever and ever. Amen.

CPSIA information can be obtained
at www.ICGtesting.com
Printed in the USA
LVHW042308210219
608421LV00001B/155/P